Adobe®
Photoshop® CS
Image Effects

Adobe®
Photoshop® CS
Image Effects

Ron Grebler, Dong Mi Kim, Kwang Woo Baek, and Kyung In Jang

SVP, Thomson Course Technology PTR: Andy Shafran

Publisher: Stacy L. Hiquet

Senior Marketing Manager: Sarah O'Donnell

Marketing Manager: Heather Hurley

Manager of Editorial Services: Heather Talbot

Senior Acquisitions Editor: Kevin Harreld

Senior Editor: Mark Garvey

Associate Marketing Managers: Kristin Eisenzopf and Sarah Dubois

Project Editor/Copy Editor: Cathleen D. Snyder

Technical Reviewers: Jeff Schwartz and Burt LaFontaine

Thomson Course Technology PTR Market Coordinator: Amanda Weaver

Interior Layout Tech: Bill Hartman

Cover Designer: Mike Tanamachi

CD-ROM Producer: Brandon Penticuff

Indexer: Sharon Shock

ISBN: 1-59200-364-8

Library of Congress Catalog Card Number: 2004105648

Printed in the United States of America

04 05 06 07 08 BU 10 9 8 7 6 5 4 3 2 1

THOMSON

COURSE TECHNOLOGY

Professional ■ Trade ■ Reference

MUSKA LIPMAN Publishing

Thomson Course Technology PTR, a division of Thomson Course Technology
25 Thomson Place ■ Boston, MA 02210 ■ http://www.courseptr.com

Effect 1
Cyber City   1

Effect 2
Broken Wall Texture   13

Effect 3
Fragments of Light   25

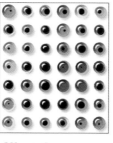

Effect 4
42 Beads   35

Effect 5
Rough Drawing Style   45

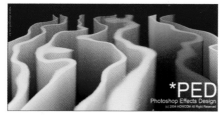

Effect 6
Separate Ways   59

Effect 7
Deep Blue Sea   69

Effect 8
Soft Sky   81

Effect 9
Woodcut Style Photograph   91

Contents

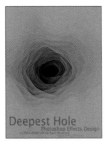

Effect 10
Deepest Hole   99

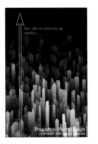

Effect 11
Skyscraper City   109

Effect 12
The Light Cube   119

Effect 13
Creative Artwork   129

Effect 14
A Cubic Pipe   147

Effect 15
Engraving Collage   159

Effect 16
Basic Photo Repair   173

Effect 17
3D Metallic Spheres   185

Effect 18
A Cube Mosaic   197

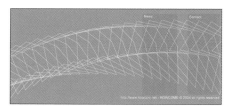

Effect 19
Wire frame Bridge   209

Effect 20
Smile face   219

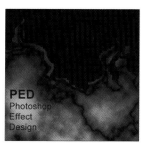

Effect 21
Realistic flame   229

Index   237

Photoshop Effects Design

P.E.D

Effect 1: Cyber City

In this section, you will use the Cutout filter to create an image with overlapping vertical bars of different shapes and sizes. This is a very simple way to create an effect that is representative of cyberspace.

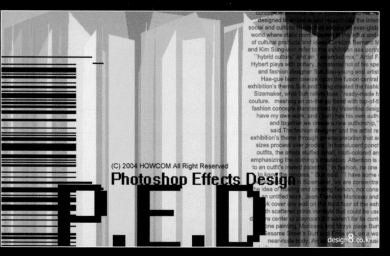

Cyber City

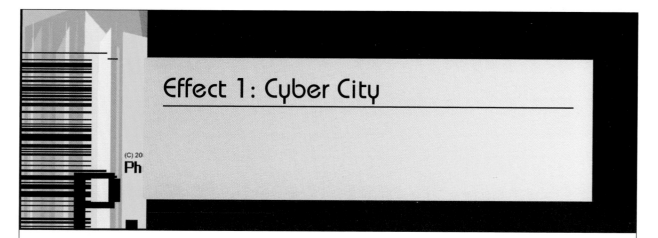

Effect 1: Cyber City

Total Steps

STEP 1.   Creating a New Work Window

STEP 2.   Setting Up the Gradient

STEP 3.   Applying the Gradient

STEP 4.   Enlarging the Image

STEP 5.   Cutting Out Stripes from the Desired Area

STEP 6.   Creating Stripes with Irregular Edges

STEP 7.   Cropping Desired Areas

STEP 8.   Applying Noise to a New Layer

STEP 9.   Creating a Selection Area of Horizontal Stripes

STEP 10.   Making Vertical Stripes

STEP 11.   Selecting a Good Spot

STEP 12.   Creating a Barcode Window

STEP 13.   Enlarging the Image

STEP 14.   Sharpening the Barcode Image

STEP 15.   Blending the Barcode Image

STEP 16.   Arranging the Barcode

STEP 17.   Entering a Title

STEP 18.   Making the Background Texture Using Small Text

STEP 19.   Wrapping Up

STEP 1. Creating a New Work Window

Press Ctrl+N to create a new work window. Set both the Width and Height to 600 to create a 600×600-pixel workspace, and then click on OK.

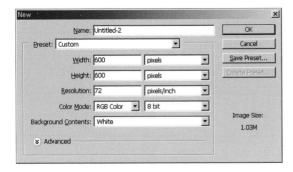

STEP 2. Setting Up the Gradient

Choose the Gradient Tool from the toolbox and click on the Linear Gradient button in the option bar at the top to create a linear gradient.

Click on the Gradient Color button to open the Gradient Editor Panel. In the center of the panel, set the Gradient Type to Noise and the Roughness to 100%. Click on the Randomize button at the bottom until you arrive at the desired gradient. Then click on OK.

Keep in mind that clicking on the Randomize button results in a random gradient, so your results will likely be different than what you see here. Also

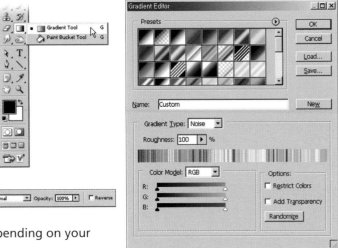

note that the presets in the Gradient Editor Panel may vary, depending on your installation of the program.

STEP 3. Applying the Gradient

Using the Gradient Tool you configured in the previous step, click on the top part of the work window and drag down to the bottom part of the window before you release the mouse. Hold down the Shift key as you drag to create a perfectly straight vertical gradient.

STEP 4. Enlarging the Image

Choose Image > Image Size from the menu at the top and set both Width and Height to 1000 percent and the Resample Image option to Nearest Neighbor. This will increase the image 10 times.

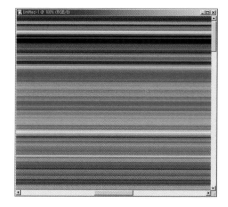

STEP 5. Cutting Out Stripes from the Desired Area

Drag the work window up and down while holding down the spacebar. A hand icon will appear, allowing you to scroll through the work window. Scroll through the image until you get to a part of it that you like.

Use the Rectangular Marquee Tool from the toolbox to select the desired area, and then

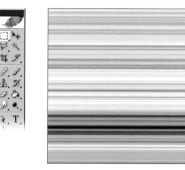

choose Image > Crop from the menu at the top to cut out the selected area.

STEP 6. Creating Stripes with Irregular Edges

Choose Filter > Artistic > Cutout from the menu at the top and set the Number of Levels to 5, the Edge Simplicity to 7, and the Edge Fidelity to 1. The stripes will be blended as a simple color with irregular edges to create a very unusual effect.

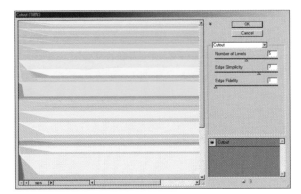

STEP 7. Cropping Desired Areas

Choose Edit > Transform > Rotate 90 CCW from the menu at the top to rotate the image 90 degrees counterclockwise, and then use the Rectangular Marquee Tool to select the area you need. Choose Image > Crop from the menu at the top to cut out the selected area.

Choose Image > Adjustments > Curves from the menu at the top and adjust the curve to sharpen the image colors, as shown here.

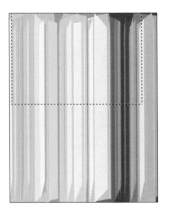
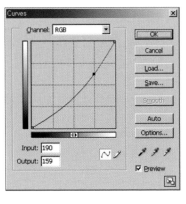
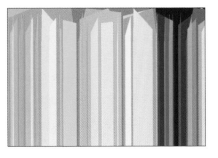

STEP 8. Applying Noise to a New Layer

Click on the Create a New Layer button at the bottom of the Layers Palette to create a new layer.

In the toolbox, click on the Default Foreground and Background Colors button

to set up the default color. Set the foreground color to black and the background color to white, and then press Ctrl+Del to fill the new layer with the background color (white).

Choose Filter > Noise > Add Noise from the menu at the top and set the Amount to 193% and the Distribution to Gaussian. Then, check Monochromatic. This will apply black and white noise to the entire image.

STEP 9. Creating a Selection Area of Horizontal Stripes

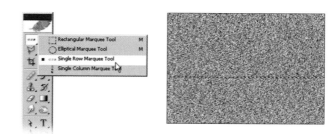

Choose the Single Row Marquee Tool from the toolbox and click on a random area of the work window to create a horizontal selection frame one-pixel thick.

STEP 10. Making Vertical Stripes

Press and hold Ctrl+Alt and the down arrow key on the keyboard for a while to copy one-pixel stripes in the vertical direction. This will create the irregular image of vertical lines shown here.

STEP 11. Selecting a Good Spot

Using the Rectangular Marquee Tool from the toolbox, drag over the part of the stripes image that looks best, and then press Ctrl+C to copy the selection.

STEP 12. Creating a Barcode Window

Press Ctrl+N to create a new work window. The new work window will automatically be set to the size of the selected image. Press Ctrl+V to paste the copied image.

STEP 13. Enlarging the Image

Choose Image > Image Size from the menu at the top and set both Width and Height to 200 percent and the Resample Image option to Nearest Neighbor. This will quadruple the size of the image (by doubling both the width and the height).

STEP 14. Sharpening the Barcode Image

Choose Image > Adjustments > Levels from the menu at the top and move the black and white tabs of the histogram close together to eliminate the gray areas in the image. Drag the background layer to the Delete Layer button at the bottom of the Layers Palette to delete it.

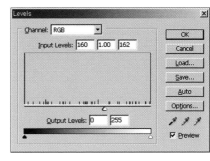

Using the Magic Wand Tool, select each white area in the barcode layer and press the Delete key. This will clear the white areas and leave only the black areas remaining.

Press Ctrl+A to select the entire image, and then press Ctrl+C to copy the completed barcode.

STEP 15. Blending the Barcode Image

Select the work window of the first image, and drag and drop the barcode layer onto the Delete Layer button at the bottom of the Layers Palette to delete it. Then press Ctrl+V to paste the copied image into the new layer.

STEP 16. Arranging the Barcode

Press Ctrl+T to apply the Free Transform command. Drag the handles around the image to rotate the image 90 degrees. Hold down the Shift key to rotate the image exactly 90 degrees. Use the Rectangular Marquee Tool to select portions of the image, and then copy and paste them complete the barcode image, as shown here.

STEP 17. Entering a Title

Click the Horizontal Type Tool from the toolbox on the work window and type in the title.

Use two separate layers to create the two different sizes of text.

Choose the font and font color in the Character Palette.

STEP 18. Making the Background Texture Using Small Text

Small text, in paragraph format, can make an excellent background texture. Drag the Horizontal Type Tool over the right part of the image to create a text field, as shown here.

Then, choose a small font size from the Character Palette and type in some text. Text used as the background (as in this example) is used more for effect than for relaying a message. If you are at a loss as to what to write, simply look up something on the Internet and copy and paste a rather lengthy bit of text from a related Web site.

STEP 19. Wrapping Up

Use the Horizontal Type Tool to type in the remaining text to finish your work. If the final image looks too spread out, rearrange the elements on the image and use the Crop Tool to crop the top and bottom parts of the image.

Effect 2: Broken Wall Texture

You can use various filters to create a faded, old texture of crumbling bricks covered with piles of dirt and dust. You can blend the text naturally to make it a part of the texture.

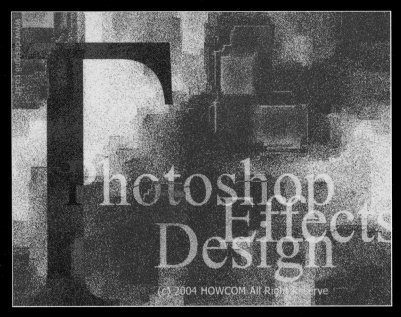

Broken Wall Texture

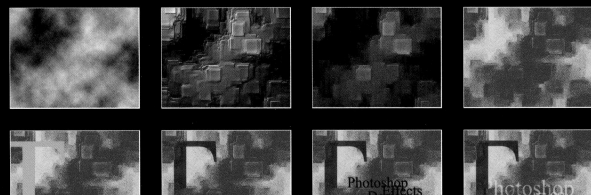

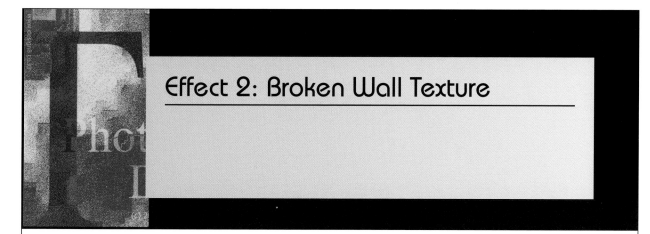

Effect 2: Broken Wall Texture

Total Steps

STEP 1.   Creating a New Work Window

STEP 2.   Making Clouds

STEP 3.   Creating Fine Particles

STEP 4.   Enlarging the Darker Areas

STEP 5.   Enlarging the Lighter Areas

STEP 6.   Softly Blending Similar Colors

STEP 7.   Sharpening the Edges of the Image

STEP 8.   3D Effects

STEP 9.   Using Filters to Blend Effects

STEP 10.   Softening the Image

STEP 11.   Blending Noise

STEP 12.   Coloring the Image

STEP 13.   Entering Text

STEP 14.   Enlarging the Text

STEP 15.   Blending Text

STEP 16.   Entering a Title

STEP 17.   Overlapping a Title

STEP 18.   Adjusting the Size of the Text

STEP 19.   Blending the Title

STEP 20.   Entering the Remaining Text

STEP 1. Creating a New Work Window

Press Ctrl+N to create a new work window. Click on the Preset box and choose 640×480 to create a 640×480-pixel workspace, and then click on OK.

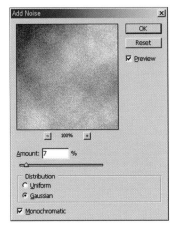

STEP 2. Making Clouds

Choose Filter > Render > Clouds from the menu at the top to create irregular black and white clouds. Press Ctrl+F to apply the command again. Every time the command is repeated, a different cloud shape will be created. Continue repeating the command until you arrive at the shape you like.

STEP 3. Creating Fine Particles

Choose Filter > Noise > Add Noise from the menu bar at the top and set the Amount to 7% and the Distribution to Gaussian, and check Monochromatic. This will create fine particles on the clouds.

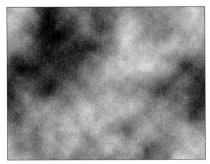

STEP 4. Enlarging the Darker Areas

Choose Filter > Other > Minimum from the menu bar at the top and set the Radius to 6 pixels. The colored particles in the darker areas of the image will become larger squares.

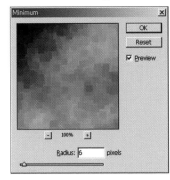

STEP 5. Enlarging the Lighter Areas

Choose Filter > Other > Maximum from the menu bar at the top and set the Radius to 26 pixels. This will enlarge the lighter areas of the image. The squares will look like they are piled onto one another and will create a 3D effect.

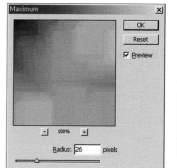

STEP 6. Softly Blending Similar Colors

Choose Filter > Blur > Smart Blur from the menu bar at the top and set the Radius to 30 and the Threshold to 30. The edges between sharply contrasting colors will remain pronounced and the image will become softer.

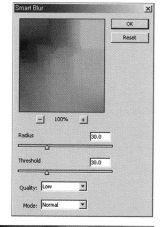

STEP 7. Sharpening the Edges of the Image

Choose Filter > Sharpen > Unsharp Mask from the menu bar at the top and set the Amount to 200%, the Radius to 15 pixels, and the Threshold to 3 levels. This will make the edges of the images sharper.

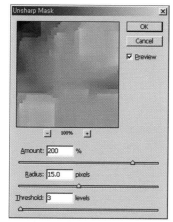

STEP 8. 3D Effects

Choose Filter > Render > Lighting Effects from the menu at the top and adjust the graph on the left side of the panel, as shown here. The line in the center shows the direction of the light. As the rounded border becomes more elongated, the angle at which the light shines becomes smaller. Drag the handles at the edges to adjust the angle and direction of light, and drag the handles in the center to adjust where the light shines. On the bot-

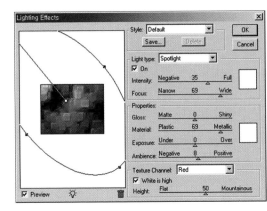 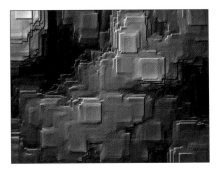

tom-right of the panel, set the Texture Channel to Red to create dimensionality. The overlapping squares now will look more like a stack of bricks. However, the 3D effect is too strong.

STEP 9. Using Filters to Blend Effects

After you apply the Lighting Effects filter, choose Edit > Fade Lighting Effects from the menu at the top and set the Opacity to 70% and the Mode to Multiply to blend the effect naturally.

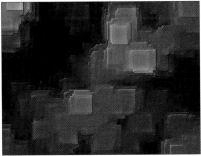

STEP 10. Softening the Image

Choose Filter > Blur > Smart Blur from the menu at the top and set the Radius to 30 and the Threshold to 30. The edges between sharply contrasting colors will remain pronounced and the image will become softer.

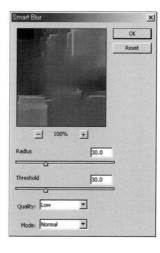

STEP 11. Blending Noise

Choose Filter > Noise > Add Noise from the menu at the top and set the Amount to 6% and the Distribution to Gaussian, and check Monochromatic. This will blend the black and white noise particles in the image.

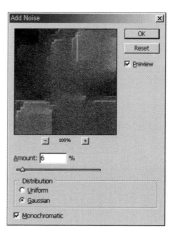

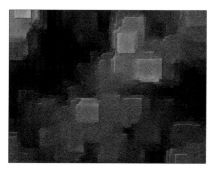

STEP 12. Coloring the Image

Click on the Create New Fill or Adjustment Layer button at the bottom of the Layers Palette and choose Gradient Map.

Click on the gradient in the Gradient Used for Grayscale Mapping box of the Gradient Map dialog box to open the Gradient Preset Panel, and choose the gradient shown here (Yellow, Violet, Orange, Blue).

The selected gradient color will be applied to the image and a new effect layer (Gradient Map) will be created in the Layers Palette.

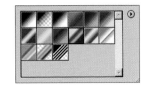 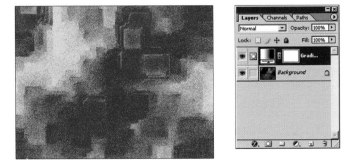

STEP 13. Entering Text

Click on the Create a New Layer button in the Layers Palette.

Click on the Foreground Color button and set the foreground color to orange (RGB=245, 110, 11).

Click the Horizontal Type Tool on the work window and type in a T.

Press Ctrl+Enter when you are finished entering text, and then adjust the font and font size of the text in the Character Palette.

STEP 14. Enlarging the Text

Press Ctrl+T to apply the Free Transform command. Drag out the handles around the text to make it larger, as shown here. Then, position the text on the left side of the image.

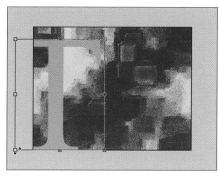

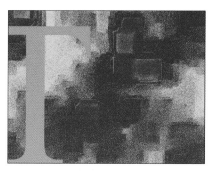

STEP 15. Blending Text

In the Layers Palette, set the Blend Mode of the text layer to Difference. A different background color will be reflected (depending on the color of the text) to create a natural blending.

STEP 16. Entering a Title

Create a new layer. Click on the Foreground Color button to set it to black, and then use the Horizontal Type Tool from the toolbox to type in the title, as shown here.

Press Ctrl+Enter when you are finished entering text, and then click the tool on another area to enter the title into a new layer. You should have a total of three title layers.

Use the Character Palette to adjust the text font, if necessary.

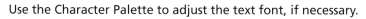

STEP 17. Overlapping a Title

Drag up the titles a little at a time so that they overlap.

In the Layers Palette, set the Blend Mode of the three layers to Multiply and the Fill to 50%.

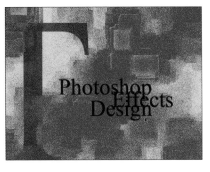

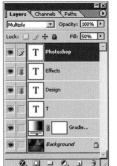

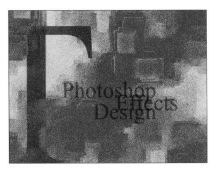

STEP 18. Adjusting the Size of the Text

Click on one of the title layers in the Layers Palette. Then, hold down the Shift key while you click on the link icons of the other two title layers to link all three title layers together.

Press Ctrl+T to apply the Free Transform command and drag out the handles in the corners of the text to make it larger. Arrange the titles as shown here.

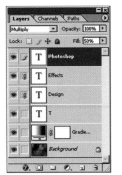

STEP 19. Blending the Title

In the Layers Palette, move the three title layers below the effect layer (Gradient Map). The text image will become the same color as the background to blend together naturally.

STEP 20. Entering the Remaining Text

Create a new layer, and then choose the Horizontal Type Tool from the toolbox. Type in the remaining text using an appropriate foreground color.

Choose the font and font size in the Character Palette, as shown here.

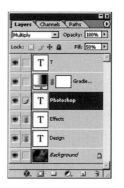

Perfume
PHOTOSHOP*EFFECTS*DESIGN

(C) 2004 HOWCOM All Right Reserved. Powered by design8

Effect 3: Fragments of Light

You will employ computer graphics using light effects to create the effect of dancing lights.

Fragments of Light

 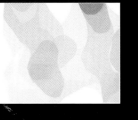 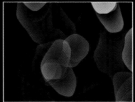 

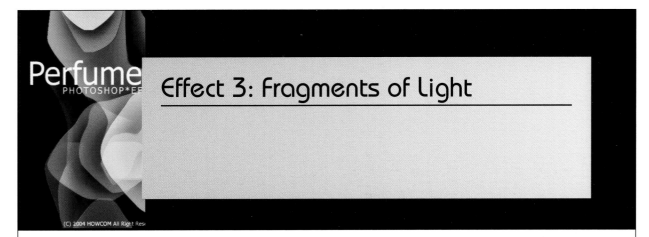

Effect 3: Fragments of Light

(C) 2004 HOWCOM All Right Rese

Total Steps

STEP 1.   Creating a New Work Window

STEP 2.   Creating Bright Particles

STEP 3.   Creating Large Colored Particles

STEP 4.   Mixing Colors in the Particles

STEP 5.   Inverting Colors

STEP 6.   Softening the Particles

STEP 7.   Sharpening the Image

STEP 8.   Creating a Color Correction Layer for the Particles

STEP 9.   Blending the Effect Layer

STEP 10. Making the Image Brighter

STEP 11. Entering a Title

STEP 12. Entering the Remaining Text

STEP 13. Copying the Effect Layer

STEP 14. Creating an Effect Layer Mask

STEP 15. Adjusting the Color of the Hidden Section

STEP 1. Creating a New Work Window

Press Ctrl+N to create a new work window. Click on the Preset box and choose 640×480 to create a 640×480-pixel workspace, and then click on OK.

STEP 2. Creating Bright Particles

Choose Filter > Texture > Grain from the menu bar at the top and set the Intensity to 100, the Contrast to 100, and the Grain Type to Clumped. Multi-colored particles will be scattered on the white background.

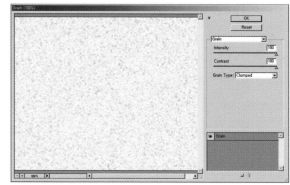

STEP 3. Creating Large Colored Particles

In the toolbox, click on the Default Foreground and Background Colors button to set up the default colors. (Set the foreground color to black and the background color to white.)

Choose Filter > Pixelate > Pointillize from the menu bar at the top and set the Cell Size to 170. Large, colored radial particles will overlap with one another.

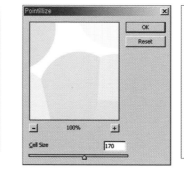

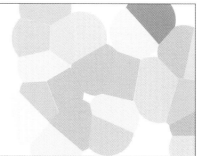

STEP 4. Mixing Colors in the Particles

Choose Filter > Noise > Median from the menu bar at the top and set the Radius to 93 pixels. The particle clumps will overlap and their colors will spread out.

STEP 5. Inverting Colors

Press Ctrl+I to invert the image colors.

Choose Filter > Sharpen > Unsharp Mask from the menu bar at the top and set the Amount to 500%, the Radius to 42 pixels, and the Threshold to 3 levels. The edges of the colored particles will look like they're shining.

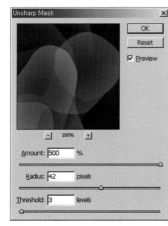

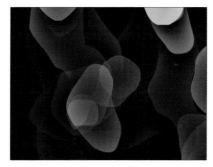

STEP 6. Softening the Particles

If you look closely, you will see wavy layers of color inside the particle clumps. Choose Filter > Blur > Smart Blur from the menu bar at the top and set the Radius to 5 and the Threshold to 18. The edges between sharply contrasting colors will remain pronounced and the image will become softer.

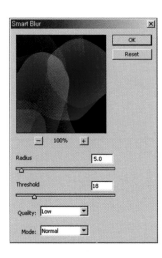

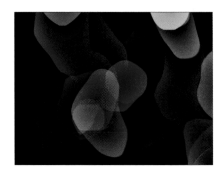

STEP 7. Sharpening the Image

Choose Image > Adjustments > Curves from the menu bar at the top and shape the curve of the graph, as shown here. Click on the center of the graph to create handles, and then, at the bottom, set the Input to 7 and the Output to 23. The dark clumps of particles will become sharper, but the colors are still not right.

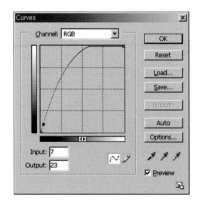

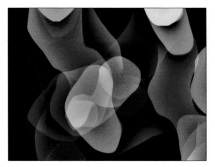

STEP 8. Creating a Color Correction Layer for the Particles

Click on the Create New Fill or Adjustment Layer button at the bottom of the Layers Palette and choose Hue/Saturation. Check Colorize and set the Hue to 0, the Saturation to 64 and the Lightness to 0.

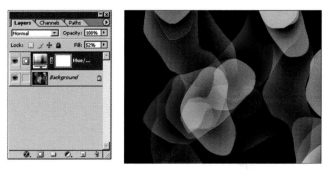

The image will become reddish in tone and a new effect layer will be created in the Layers Palette.

STEP 9. Blending the Effect Layer

Select the new effect layer from the Layers Palette and set the Fill to 52%. This will soften the red of the effect and let the original color show through naturally. However, the image will look darker now.

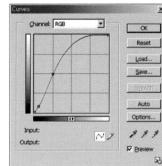

STEP 10. Making the Image Brighter

Click on the Create New Fill or Adjustment Layer button at the bottom of the Layers Palette and select Curves.

Shape the curve as shown here to make the image sharper and brighter.

STEP 11. Entering a Title

Create a new layer.

Click on the Switch Foreground and Background Colors button in the toolbox to set the foreground color to white.

Then, click the Horizontal Type Tool on the workspace and type in the desired title.

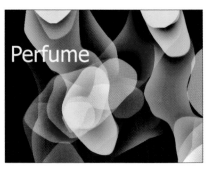

Choose the font and font size in the Character Palette, as shown here.

STEP 12. Entering the Remaining Text

Create a new layer and use the Horizontal Type Tool to create the remaining text. Overall, the brighter area in the right part of the image will take the attention away from the center.

STEP 13. Copying the Effect Layer

In the Layers Palette, drag and drop the Hue/Saturation effect layer onto the Create a New Layer Button at the bottom. Then, move the copied layer right above the Curve effect layer.

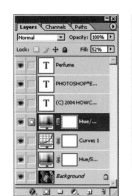

STEP 14. Creating an Effect Layer Mask

Looking at the effect layer in the Layers Palette, you can see a mask thumbnail to the right of the layer. When the mask image is edited, the layer effect can only be applied to a part of the image.

Select the Rectangular Marquee Tool from the toolbox and drag it over the right part of the image to make a selection.

Hold down the Shift key and select a thin rectangle to the left of the first selected region. This will result in two regions selected simultaneously, as shown in the figures.

Press Shift+Ctrl+I to invert the selection frame and then press Del to delete the copied mask of the effect layer. The effect layer will not be applied to the deleted section, allowing the color image below to show through.

Looking at the mask thumbnail of the selected effect layer in the Layers Palette, you can see that the deleted portion is filled in with black. Set the Fill of the selected duplicate effect layer to 80%.

STEP 15. Adjusting the Color of the Hidden Section

In the Layers Palette, double-click on the layer icon of the duplicate effect layer (Hue/Saturation).

Set the Hue to 229, the Saturation to 47, and the Lightness to –45. The hidden section will turn darker and the focus will be brought back to the center of the image.

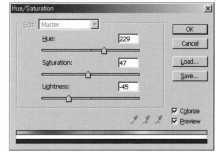

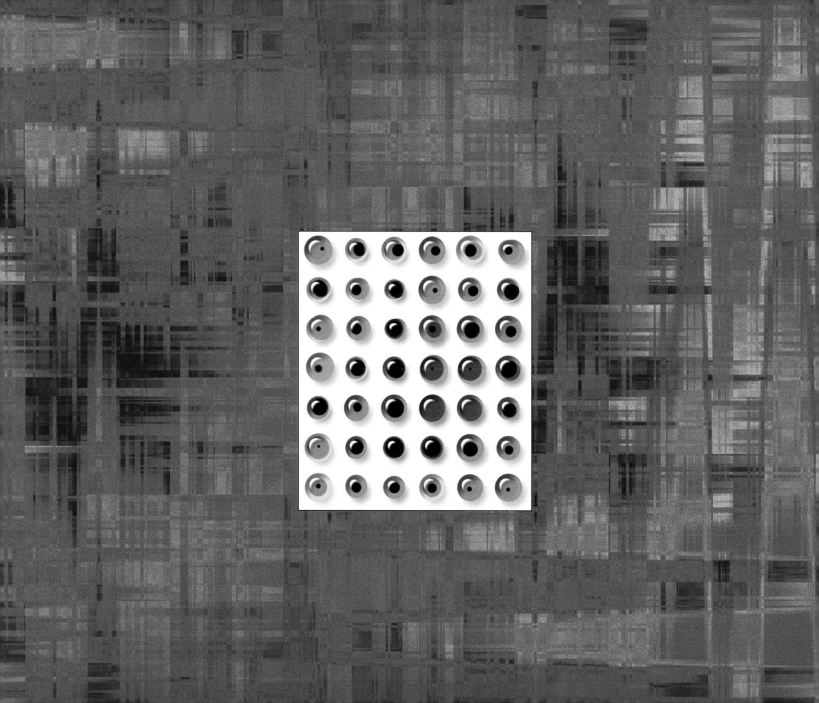

Effect 4: 42 Beads

Colorful beads of different shapes, sizes, and colors are arranged together in this fun and interesting image. The Color Halftone command is usually used to portray the halftone dots that appear in the final printout, but in this example, it is used to create a fun and interesting effect.

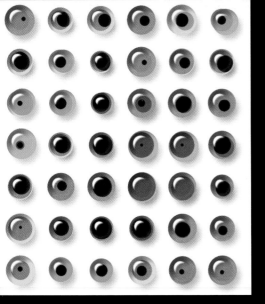

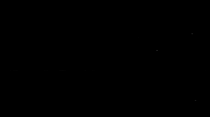

36

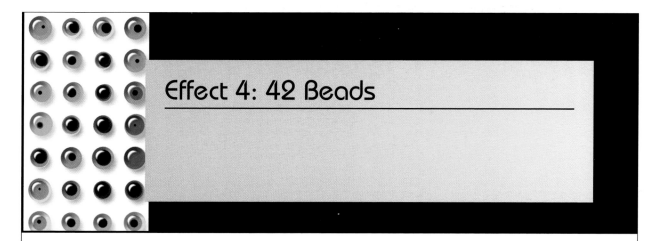

Effect 4: 42 Beads

Total Steps

STEP 1.   Creating a New Work Window

STEP 2.   Spraying Colorful Dots

STEP 3.   Creating Rectangular Mosaic Tiles

STEP 4.   Sharpening the Mosaic Color

STEP 5.   Enlarging the Image

STEP 6.   Drawing Beads

STEP 7.   Cutting Out the Necessary Areas

STEP 8.   Making a White Background Layer

STEP 9.   Deleting the White Background

STEP 10.   Copying the Water Drop Layer Style

STEP 11.   3D Beads

STEP 12.   Turning Off Unnecessary Styles

STEP 13.   Creating Color Shadows for the Beads

STEP 14.   Making the Shadow Smaller

STEP 15.   Blending the Shadow

STEP 16.   Entering the Title

STEP 17.   Entering the Remaining Text

STEP 1. Creating a New Work Window

Press Ctrl+N to create a new work window. Click on the Preset box and choose 640×480 to create a 640×480-pixel workspace, and then click on OK.

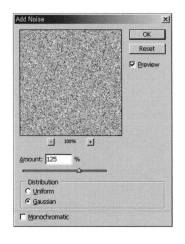

STEP 2. Spraying Colorful Dots

Choose Filter > Noise > Add Noise from the menu bar at the top and set the Amount to 125% and the Distribution to Gaussian. Colorful dots will be sprayed over the entire image.

STEP 3. Creating Rectangular Mosaic Tiles

Choose Filter > Pixelate > Mosaic from the menu bar at the top and set the Cell Size to 40 square. This will create a 40-pixel rectangular mosaic pattern on the window. However, as you can see here, the color of the mosaic is almost gray.

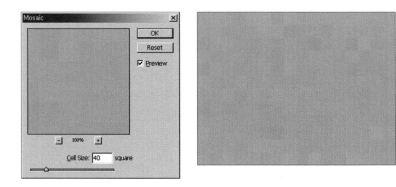

STEP 4. Sharpening the Mosaic Color

Choose Image > Adjustments >
Hue/Saturation from the menu bar at the top
and set the Lightness to 40 and the Saturation
to 100. Adjust the Hue slider until you get the
color you want. An image with lots of red and
orange is best. The color of the mosaic will
now be more intense.

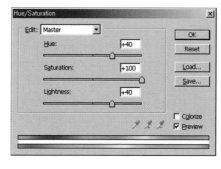 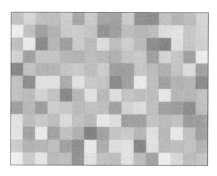

STEP 5. Enlarging the Image

Choose Image > Image Size from the menu at
the top and set both the Width and Height to
300 percent to triple the size of the image.
The image will be enlarged and each square
in the mosaic will be 120 pixels wide.

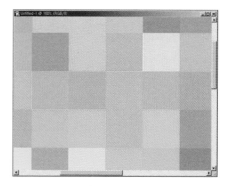

STEP 6. Drawing Beads

Choose Filter >
Pixelate > Color
Halftone from the
menu bar at the
top and set the
Max. Radius to 60
Pixels and the Screen Angles to 1/0/0/0.

In the cyan channel image, which is the first
channel, the image will turn off-kilter to create
a bead with a radius of 60 pixels.

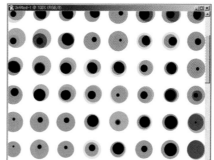 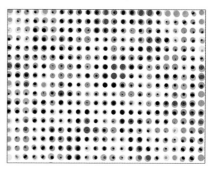

STEP 7. Cutting Out the Necessary Areas

Drag the Rectangular Marquee Tool over the beads that are shaped and arranged the way you want to select them.

Then, choose Image > Crop from the top to cut out the selected area. Here we have cropped a section of six beads across and seven beads down.

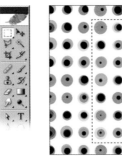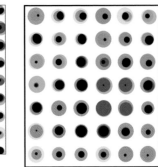

STEP 8. Making a White Background Layer

Press Ctrl+J to make a copy of the image layer, and then choose the Background layer from the bottom of the Layers Palette.

In the toolbox, click on the Default Foreground and Background Colors button to set up the default color. Set the foreground color to black and the background color to white. Press Ctrl+Del to fill in the background layer with the background color (white).

Click on the bead image layer at the top of the Layers Palette to select it.

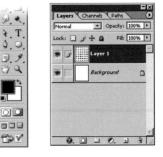

STEP 9. Deleting the White Background

Choose the Magic Wand Tool from the toolbox.

Go to the option bar at the top and set the Tolerance to 10.

Click the tool on the white background of the image so that the entire white background is selected, and then press Del to delete the selected background.

Press Ctrl+J to make another copy of the selected layer. You can see that this new layer has been added to the Layers Palette.

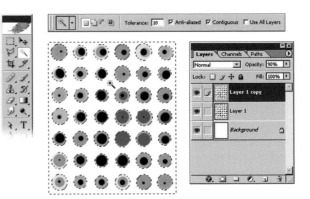

STEP 10. Copying the Water Drop Layer Style

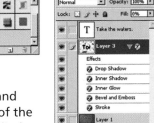

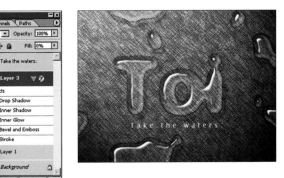

Go to the Styles Palette and click on the water drop style icon (the one you made in a previous example) to apply it to the bead image layer.

Select the water drop text layer from the Layers Palette, and then click on the Create New Style button at the bottom of the Styles Palette to save the water drop style, which was applied to the selected layer, to the Styles Palette.

STEP 11. 3D Beads

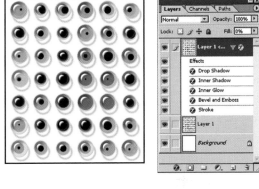

The water drop style has been applied to the bead image to create a realistic and transparent 3D effect.

Looking at the Layers Palette, you can see that the water drop style has been applied to the bead image layer and the style is registered below the respective layer.

STEP 12. Turning Off Unnecessary Styles

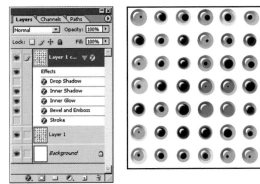

Looking at the bead layer in the Layers Palette, you will notice different layer effects applied to the layer (such as Drop Shadow and Stroke). Click on the Layer Visibility icon to turn off the layer effects that you don't need.

STEP 13. Creating Color Shadows for the Beads

Choose the bead image layer from the bottom of the Layers Palette, and then click on the Layer Visibility icon of the bead layer right above it to hide it from view.

Choose Filter > Blur > Gaussian Blur from the menu at the top and set the Radius to 7 pixels. This will blur the bead image.

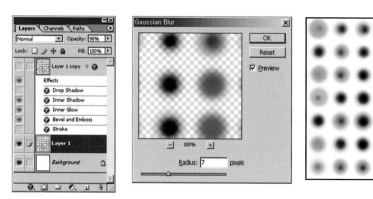

STEP 14. Making the Shadow Smaller

Click on the layer that you have selected in the Layers Palette while holding down the Ctrl key to create a selection frame in the shape of the selected layer.

Press Shift+Ctrl+I to invert the selection frames, and then press Del to delete the selection. This will remove some of the blurred areas around the selected beads to make the shadow smaller. Press Ctrl+D to deselect the selection.

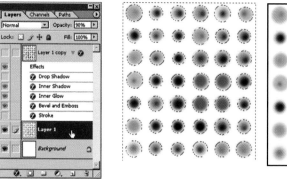
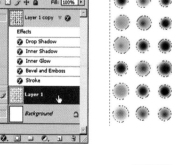

STEP 15. Blending the Shadow

Click on the Layer Visibility icon of the top bead image layer that was hidden in a previous step so that it is visible again. Then, select the bottom bead image layer and set the Blend Mode to Linear Burn and the Fill to 50%. Hold down the Ctrl key and press the right arrow and down arrow keys on the keyboard a couple of times so that the color shadow overlaps with the beads, as shown here.

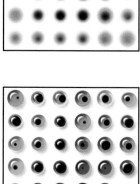

STEP 16. Entering the Title

Use the Horizontal Type Tool from the tool-box to type in the title.

Then, adjust the font and font size in the Character Palette.

In the Layers Palette, drag the text layer between the two bead layers and then set the Blend Mode of the text layer to Linear Burn and the Fill to 50%. This will make it look like the text is written on the white base below the bead. You can even have the bead cover a portion of the text to emphasize the 3D effect.

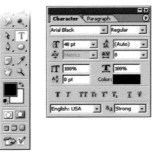

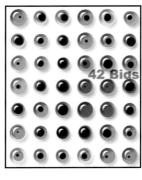

STEP 17. Entering the Remaining Text

Choose the Horizontal Type Tool from the toolbox and type in the remaining text. Move the remaining text between the two bead layers and adjust the Blend Mode and Fill as you did for the title.

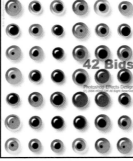
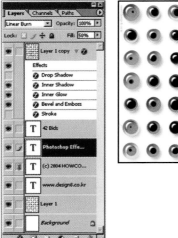

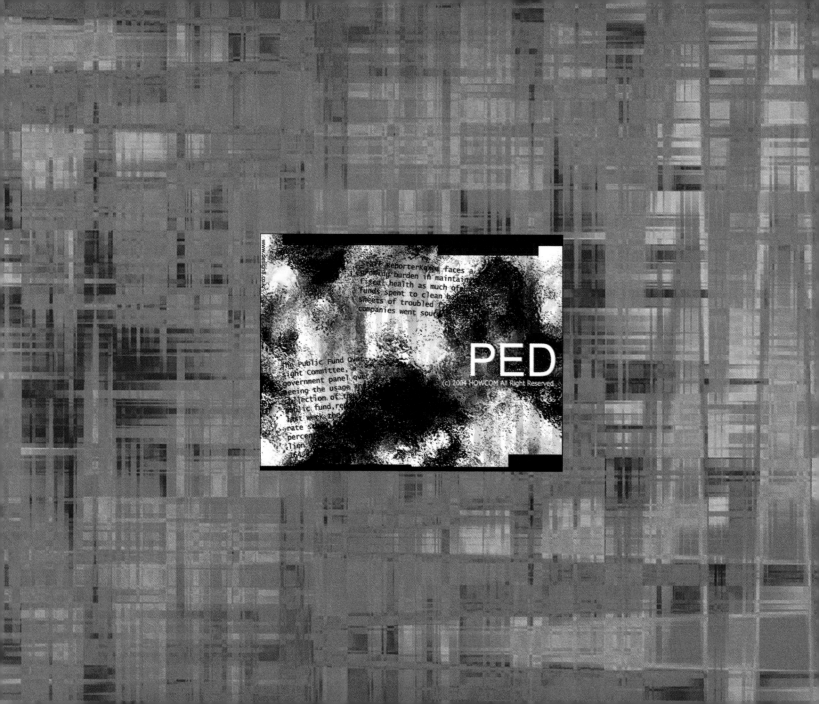

Effect 5: Rough Drawing Style

You will roughly brush black ink and watercolors onto a piece of paper to create a texture that looks hand-drawn. You can use various filters and effects in a number of ways to roughen an image to create different effects.

Rough Drawing Style

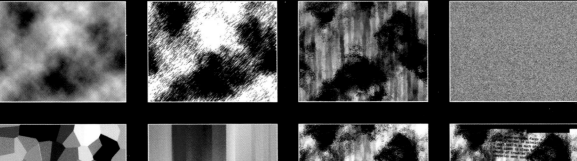

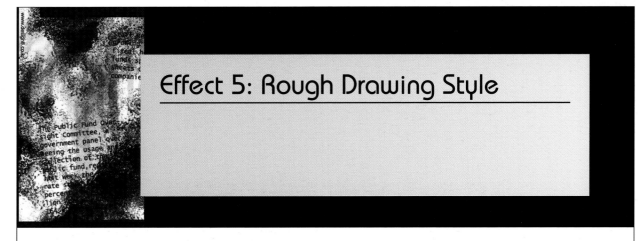

Effect 5: Rough Drawing Style

Total Steps

STEP 1.   Creating a New Work Window

STEP 2.   Transforming the Clouds

STEP 3.   Adjusting the Shadows in the Clouds

STEP 4.   Using the Filter Gallery

STEP 5.   Applying Various Filters at Once

STEP 6.   Saving the Displace Map Image

STEP 7.   Making Clouds

STEP 8.   Making a Pen Sketch

STEP 9.   Blurring the Image

STEP 10. Applying the Displace Command

STEP 11. Applying the Displace Command Again

STEP 12. Creating Fibers

STEP 13. Blurring the Image

STEP 14. Making Runny Paint

STEP 15. Blending the Texture

STEP 16. Creating a Small Colored Dot Layer

STEP 17. Making the Colored Dots Bigger

STEP 18. Correcting the Image Color

STEP 19. Making Vertical Stripes

STEP 20. Blurring the Image

STEP 21. Applying Color to the Texture

STEP 22. Darkening the Black Texture

STEP 23. Entering the Texture Text

STEP 24. Making a Black Border

STEP 25. Entering a Title

STEP 1. Creating a New Work Window

Press Ctrl+N to create a new work window. Click on the Preset box and choose 640×480 to create a 640×480-pixel workspace, and then click on OK.

In the toolbox, click on the Default Foreground and Background Colors button to set up the default color.

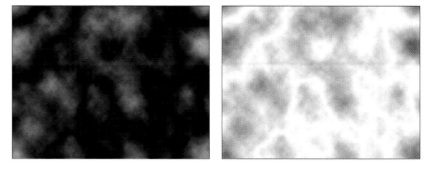

Set the foreground color to black and the background color to white. Choose Filter > Render > Clouds from the menu at the top to create irregular black and white clouds. Press Ctrl+F to apply the command again. Every time the command is repeated, a different cloud shape will be created. Continue repeating the command until you arrive at the shape you want.

STEP 2. Transforming the Clouds

Choose Filter > Render > Difference Clouds from the menu at the top. Press Ctrl+F to apply the command again. Continue repeating the command until you arrive at the shape you want. Press Ctrl+I to invert the image colors.

STEP 3. Adjusting the Shadows in the Clouds

Choose Image > Adjustments > Levels and move the black tab below the histogram to the right, near the point where the graph starts. The darker areas of the cloud image will appear blacker.

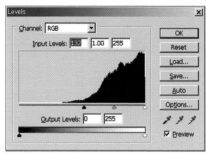

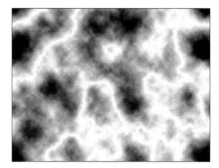

STEP 4. Using the Filter Gallery

The Filter Gallery in Photoshop CS allows you to use filters as you would layers. You can apply many filters at the same time and even change their order, view, and settings. Not all filters are supported by the Filter Gallery, but those that are will automatically open in the Filter Gallery window. Choose Filter > Artistic > Palette Knife from the menu at the top to open the Filter Gallery. Set the Stroke Size to 20, the Stroke Detail to 3, and the Softness to 0. You can see a preview of what your image will look like with the filter in the preview window on the left. Leave the Filter Gallery open and move on to the next step.

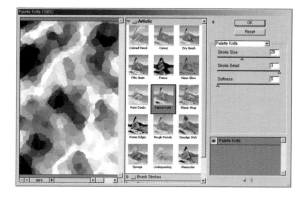

STEP 5. Applying Various Filters at Once

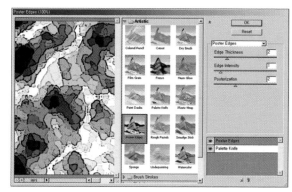

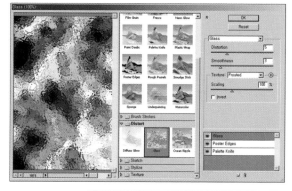

With the Filter Gallery still open, click on the New Effect Layer button to make a new filter layer. Click on the Poster Edges thumbnail from the middle of the filter list to apply the filter, and then set the Edge Thickness to 2, Edge Intensity to 1, and Posterization to 2. This filter will create a poster edge to the image.

Click on the New Effect Layer button again, and this time select the Glass filter. Set the Distortion to 5, Smoothness to 3, Texture to Frosted, and Scaling to 100%. The three filters will overlap. Click on OK.

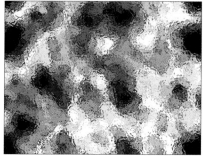

STEP 6. Saving the Displace Map Image

The completed image will be used as the Displace map. Press Ctrl+S to save the completed image as a PSD file (disp_map3.psd). This file is included on the supplementary CD-ROM.

STEP 7. Making Clouds

Now you can start making the actual image. Press Ctrl+N to create a new 640×480-pixel file, and then choose Filter > Render > Clouds from the menu at the top to create irregular black and white clouds. Press Ctrl+F to apply the command again. Every time the command is repeated, a different cloud shape will be created. Continue applying the command until the black areas of the cloud are positioned the way you want.

STEP 8. Making a Pen Sketch

Choose Filter > Sketch > Graphic Pen from the menu at the top and set the Stroke Length to 15 and the Light/Dark Balance to 50. The clouds will look as if they've been sketched using a pen.

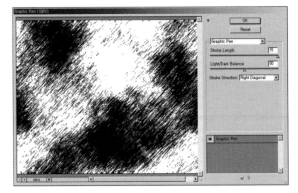

STEP 9. Blurring the Image

Choose Filter > Blur > Gaussian Blur from the menu at the top and set the Radius to 5 pixels. The image will appear blurred and the fine lines will disappear.

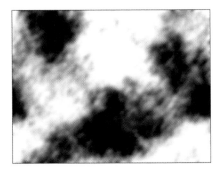

STEP 10. Applying the Displace Command

Choose Filter > Distort > Displace from the menu at the top and set the Horizontal Scale to 40 and the Vertical Scale to 40. Click on OK. In the Displace Map Source dialog box, choose the displace file you created in a previous step (disp_map3.psd). This file is included on the supplementary CD-ROM. The image will appear scattered, but the intensity of the scatter is too weak.

STEP 11. Applying the Displace Command Again

Choose Image > Rotate Canvas > 90 CW from the menu at the top to rotate the image 90 degrees clockwise. Press Ctrl+F to apply the displace map again. Because you've rotated the image, the displace map will be applied in a different direction. Choose Image > Rotate Canvas > 90 CCW from the menu at the top to move the image back to its original position.

STEP 12. Creating Fibers

Click on the Create a New Layer button at the bottom of the Layers Palette to create a new layer. Press Ctrl+Del to fill in the new layer with the background color (white).

Choose Filter > Render > Fibers from the menu at the top and set the Variance to 16 and the Strength to 4. This will create vertical fibers on the image.

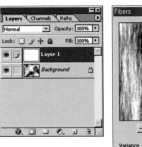
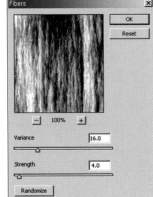
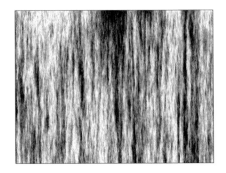

STEP 13. Blurring the Image

Choose Filter > Blur > Gaussian Blur from the menu at the top and set the Radius to 5 pixels. This will blur the rough image.

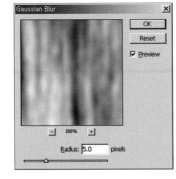
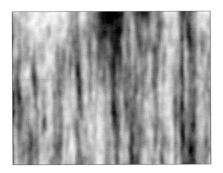

STEP 14. Making Runny Paint

Choose Filter > Artistic > Dry Brush from the menu at the top and set the Brush Size to 5, the Brush Detail to 4 and the Texture to 3.

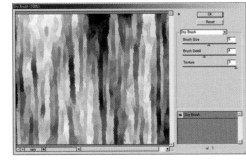
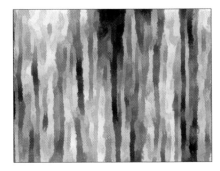

STEP 15. Blending the Texture

In the Layers Palette, set the Blend Mode of the selected layer to Multiply and the Fill to 80%. This will blend the image with the runny paint and the black texture naturally.

STEP 16. Creating a Small Colored Dot Layer

Click on the Create a New Layer button at the bottom of the Layers Palette to create a new layer. Press Ctrl+Del to fill in the new layer with the background color (white).

Choose Filter > Noise > Add Noise from the menu at the top and set the Amount to 400% and the Distribution to Gaussian. This will create many small, colored dots on the image.

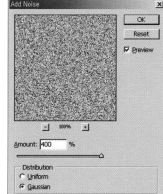

STEP 17. Making the Colored Dots Bigger

Choose Filter > Pixelate > Crystallize from the menu at the top and set the Cell Size to 100. This will create larger, irregular particles that clump together.

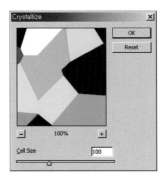

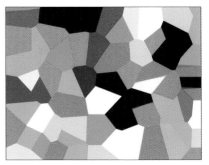

STEP 18. Correcting the Image Color

Choose Image > Adjustments > Photo Filter. Click on the Color option and set it to red (RGB=236, 0, 0). Set the Density to 85%. This will change the overall color of the dots.

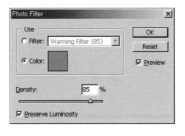

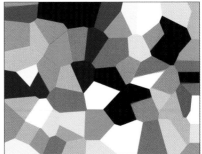

STEP 19. Making Vertical Stripes

Choose Filter > Blur > Motion Blur from the menu at the top and set the Angle to 90 and the Distance to 999 pixels. The colored dots will spread out in a vertical direction to create vertical stripes.

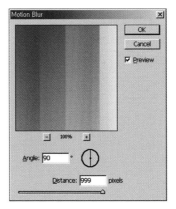

STEP 20. Blurring the Image

Choose Filter > Blur > Gaussian Blur from the menu at the top and set the Radius to 15 pixels. This will blur the image.

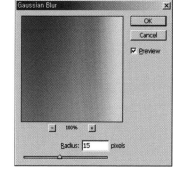

STEP 21. Applying Color to the Texture

In the Layers Palette, set the Blend Mode of the color layer to Color Dodge and the Fill to 85%. This will blend the black and white texture with the stripes. However, the image is too bright overall.

STEP 22. Darkening the Black Texture

In the Layers Palette, choose the black lump layer from the bottom (the Background layer).

Then, choose Image > Adjustments > Curves and shape the curve of the graph, as shown here. The black lump will become darker and larger.

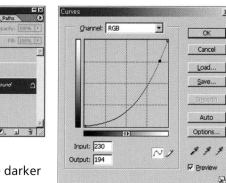

STEP 23. Entering the Texture Text

Drag the Horizontal Type Tool over the image to create an adequately sized text field and type in a line of text. Because this text will be used as texture, you should concentrate more on using the handles in the corners of the text field to adjust the size of the text than on what you type.

You can also drag on the outside of the text field to rotate the text.

Press Ctrl+Enter when you are finished editing the text.

STEP 24. Making a Black Border

Type in text here and there to complete the texture. However, as you can see, the top and bottom of the image appear too empty.

Click on the Create a New Layer button at the bottom of the Layers Palette to create a new layer.

Drag the Rectangular Marquee Tool over the top and bottom parts of the image while holding down the Shift key to make the irregular selection shown here.

Then, press Alt+Del to fill in the selection with the foreground color (black). Press Ctrl+D to deselect the selection.

STEP 25. Entering a Title

Set the foreground color to white in the toolbox, and then use the Horizontal Type Tool to type in the title, as shown here.

www.design.co.kr

*PED
Photoshop Effects Design
(c) 2004 HOWCOM All Right Reserved

Effect 6: Separate Ways

Life is all about taking different paths, such as the three-dimensional path here that disappears way off down the road.

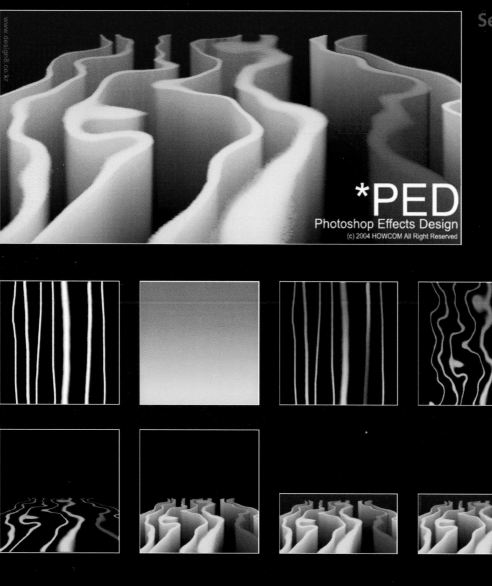

Separate Ways

*PED
Photoshop Effects Design
(c) 2004 HOWCOM All Right Reserved

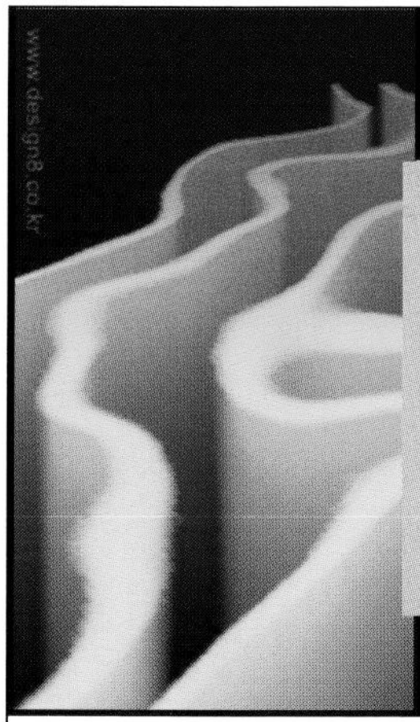

Effect 6: Separate Ways

Total Steps

STEP 1.   Creating a New Work Window

STEP 2.   Drawing White Vertical Lines

STEP 3.   Making Clouds

STEP 4.   Saving the Cloud Image as a Displace Map

STEP 5.   Making a Gradient Layer

STEP 6.   Blending the Stripe Colors

STEP 7.   Selecting One Vertical Line

STEP 8.   Changing the Color of the Selected Line

STEP 9.   Merging Layers

STEP 10.   Applying the Displace Map

STEP 11.   Adding Dimensionality

STEP 12.   Copying Layers

STEP 13.   Making a 3D Effect

STEP 14.   Resetting the Image

STEP 15.   Cutting Out the Necessary Areas

STEP 16.   Making a Gradient Layer

STEP 17.   Blending the Gradient to the Background

STEP 18.   Correcting the 3D Column Effect

STEP 19.   Entering a Title

STEP 1. Creating a New Work Window

Press Ctrl+N to create a new work window. Set both the Width and Height to 800 pixels to create a square work window, and then click on OK.

STEP 2. Drawing White Vertical Lines

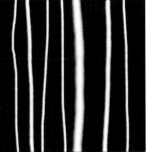

In the toolbox, click on the Default Foreground and Background Colors button to set up the default color, and then click on the Switch Foreground and Background Colors button to set the foreground color to white and the background color to black.

Press Ctrl+Del to fill in the entire work window with the background color (black), and then click on the Create a New Layer button at the bottom of the Layers Palette to create a new layer.

Click on the Brush Tool, and then view the Brush Presets panel and choose the brush shown here from the very bottom of the list. If you can't see the brush, click on the Option button, choose Reset Brush, and search for the brush.

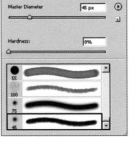

Adjust the brush size, and then drag it vertically down the work window to create the vertical stripes shown here. Don't worry about drawing perfectly straight lines. You want the lines to look natural, as they do here.

STEP 3. Making Clouds

Click on the Create a New Layer button at the bottom of the Layers Palette to create a new layer, and then choose Filter > Render > Clouds from the menu at the top to create irregular black and white clouds. Press Ctrl+F to apply the command again. Every time the command is repeated, a different cloud shape will be created. Continue to apply the command until you are satisfied with the results.

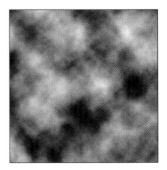

STEP 4. Saving the Cloud Image as a Displace Map

Choose Filter > Blur > Gaussian Blur from the menu at the top and set the Radius to 18 pixels. Press Ctrl+Alt+S to save a copy of the active cloud image as a PSD file (disp_map4.psd). This file is included on the supplementary CD-ROM.

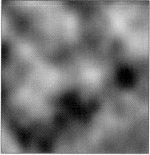
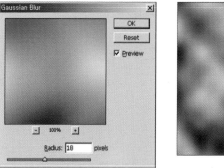

STEP 5. Making a Gradient Layer

In the Layers Palette, click on the Layer Visibility icon in front of the displace map layer to hide it from view. Then, click on the Create a New Layer button to create a new layer. Move the new layer below the displace map layer.

In the toolbox, set the foreground color to yellow (RGB=255, 240, 0) and the background color to red (RGB=218, 0, 0).

Choose the Gradient Tool, select a linear gradient with the color scheme shown, and drag the mouse from the bottom of the work window up to the top to apply the gradient. Hold down the Shift key to make a perfectly straight gradient.

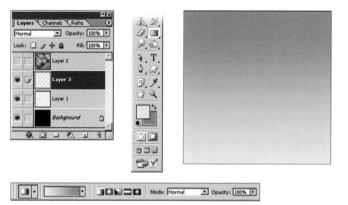

STEP 6. Blending the Stripe Colors

In the Layers Palette, set the Blend Mode of the color layer to Multiply. This will apply the gradient colors to the white stripes.

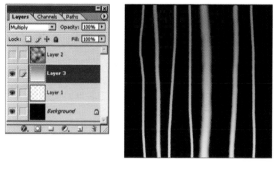

STEP 7. Selecting One Vertical Line

Drag the Rectangular Marquee Tool over one of the vertical lines to select it.

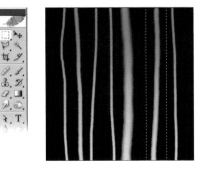

STEP 8. Changing the Color of the Selected Line

Choose Image > Adjustments > Hue/Saturation from the menu at the top and set the Hue to 180. The red line will turn blue.

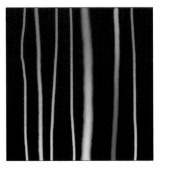

STEP 9. Merging Layers

Press Shift+Ctrl+E to merge (Merge Linked) all the visible layers. Then, press Ctrl+J to make another copy of the merged layer.

In the toolbox, click on the Default Foreground and Background Colors button to set up the default color. Set the foreground color to black and the background color to white. Then, choosing the Background layer from the very bottom of the Layers Palette, press Alt+Del to fill in the layer with the foreground color (black). Click on the stripe layer right above the Background layer.

STEP 10. Applying the Displace Map

Choose Filter > Distort > Displace from the menu at the top and set the Horizontal Scale to 100 and the Vertical Scale to 0. Click on OK. In the Displace Map Source dialog box, choose the displace file you made in a previous step (disp_map4.psd). This file is included on the supplementary CD-ROM. The displace map image will cause the stripe image to be distorted in the horizontal direction.

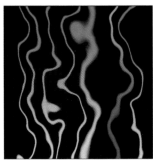

STEP 11. Adding Dimensionality

Press Ctrl+T to apply the Free Transform command. Drag on the handles around the image while you hold down the Ctrl key to create a strong 3D effect, as shown here. If you run out of room, press Ctrl+– to make the image smaller, or drag the edges of the work window to make the gray space larger.

STEP 12. Copying Layers

Press Ctrl+E to merge the stripe layer and the background layer. Then, press Ctrl+J to copy the layer. In the Layers Palette, select the Background layer, and then click on the Layer Visibility icon of the copied stripe layer right above it to hide it from view.

STEP 13. Making a 3D Effect

Choose Image > Rotate Canvas > 90 CCW to rotate the image 90 degrees counterclockwise. Choose Filter > Stylize > Wind from the menu at the top and set the Method to Wind and the Direction to From the Left.

Press Ctrl+F five to seven times to repeat the command. This will create the 3D effect shown here.

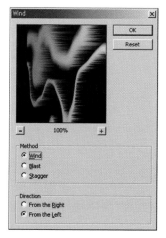

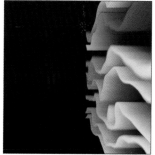

STEP 14. Resetting the Image

Choose Image > Rotate Canvas > 90 CW from the menu at the top to move the image back to its original position. Click on the copied stripe layer in the Layers Palette so that it is visible again and set the Blend Mode to Screen.

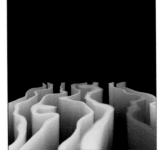 

STEP 15. Cutting Out the Necessary Areas

Drag the Crop Tool over the part of the image that you need and press Enter to crop it.

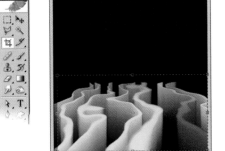 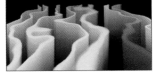

STEP 16. Making a Gradient Layer

In the toolbox, set the foreground color to dark purple and the background color to black, and then choose the Gradient Tool.

Click on the Create a New Layer button in the Layers Palette to create a new layer, and then drag the mouse from the top of the work window down to the bottom to apply the gradient. Hold down the Shift key to make a perfectly straight gradient.

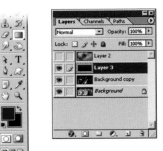

STEP 17. Blending the Gradient to the Background

In the Layers Palette, set the Blend Mode of the gradient layer to Lighten. The gradient will be applied only to areas of the background that are darker than the gradient color.

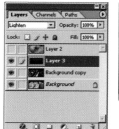
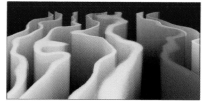

STEP 18. Correcting the 3D Column Effect

The vertical stripes take away from the 3D column effect. Select the Background layer from the very bottom of the Layers Palette and choose Filter > Blur > Motion Blur.

Set the Angle to 0 and the Distance to 6 pixels. The sides of the image will blur slightly and the rough stripes will disappear.

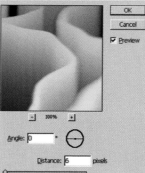
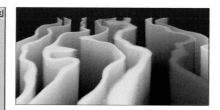

STEP 19. Entering a Title

Set the foreground color to white in the toolbox. Then, use the Horizontal Type Tool to type in the title, as shown here.

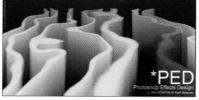

Deep
blue Sea

Effect 7: Deep Blue Sea

Looking up from the depths of the deep, blue sea, you will see the gentle ripples of the water and the sun's rays on the water's surface. Photoshop can help you create such a fantastic and mystical scene.

Deep Blue Sea

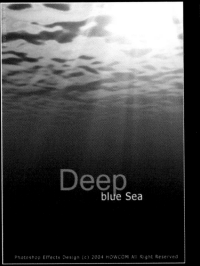

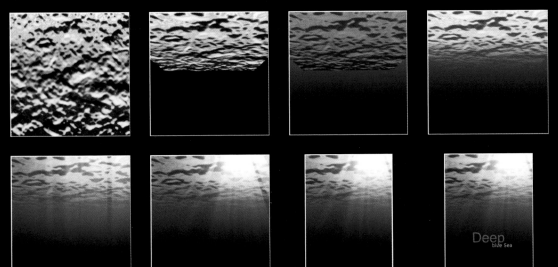

Effect 7: Deep Blue Sea

Deep
blue Sea

Photoshop Effects Design (c) 2004 HOWCOM All Righ

Total Steps

STEP 1.   Creating a New Work Window

STEP 2.   Making Cloud Textures

STEP 3.   Creating 3D Clouds

STEP 4.   Adjusting 3D Clouds

STEP 5.   Applying a Blue Gradient

STEP 6.   Blending the Water Ripples

STEP 7.   Choosing the Bottom of the Water Ripples

STEP 8.   Blurring the Bottom of the Water Ripples

STEP 9.   Shining Water Ripples

STEP 10.   Choosing the Lit Area

STEP 11.   Deleting the Other Areas

STEP 12.   Making the Sun's Rays

STEP 13.   Creating a Black Background for the Sun's Rays

STEP 14.   Sharpening the Sun's Rays Image

STEP 15.   Making the Sun's Rays Longer

STEP 16.   Brightening the Sun's Rays

STEP 17.   Blending the Sun's Rays

STEP 18.   Creating 3D Sun Rays

STEP 19.   Setting Up the Brush

STEP 20.   Lighting Up the Top-Right Part of the Image

STEP 21.   Cutting Out the Necessary Areas

STEP 22.   Entering the Title

STEP 1. Creating a New Work Window

Press Ctrl+N to create a new work window. Set both the Width and Height to 800 pixels to create a square work window, and then click on OK.

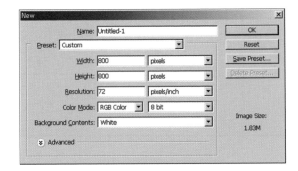

STEP 2. Making Cloud Textures

In the toolbox, click on the Default Foreground and Background Colors button to set up the default colors, and then use the Paint Bucket Tool to fill the foreground with black. Click on the Switch Foreground and Background Colors button to set the foreground color to white and the background color to black.

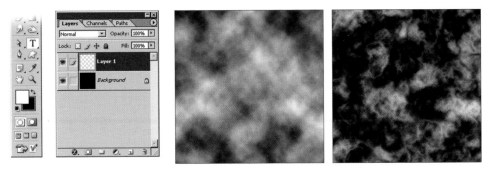

Then, click on the Create a New Layer button at the bottom of the Layers Palette to create a new layer. Choose Filter > Render > Clouds from the menu at the top to create irregular black and white clouds.

Then, select Filter > Render > Difference Clouds. Press Ctrl+F four to five times to repeat the command, until you have a rather complex-looking cloud texture, as shown here.

STEP 3. Creating 3D Clouds

Choose Filter > Sketch > Bas Relief from the menu at the top and set the Detail to 3, the Smoothness to 3, and the Light to Bottom. Click on OK in the Bas Relief dialog box to accept the changes. This will create 3D clouds.

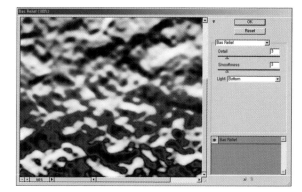 

STEP 4. Adjusting 3D Clouds

Press Ctrl+T to apply the Free Transform command. Drag on the handles around the image while you hold down the Ctrl key to create a strong 3D effect, as shown here. Then, press Enter. If you run out of room, press Ctrl+– to make the image smaller, or drag on the edges of the work window to make the gray space larger.

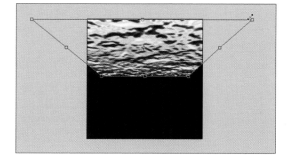 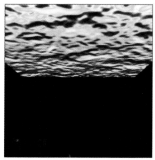

STEP 5. Applying a Blue Gradient

Choose the Background layer from the bottom of the Layers Palette and click on the Layer Visibility icon of the cloud layer (Layer 1) right above it to hide it from view.

Click on the Foreground Color button in the toolbox to set the foreground color to blue (RGB=0, 104, 170), and then click on OK to accept the changes.

Drag the mouse from the top of the window down to the bottom to apply the gradient, as shown here.

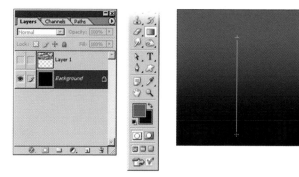

STEP 6. Blending the Water Ripples

Click on the Layer Visibility icon next to the hidden cloud layer in the Layers Palette so that it is visible again, and set the Blend Mode to Linear Light and the Fill to 32%. This will blend the two images to create the water's surface.

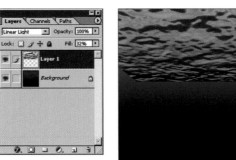

STEP 7. Choosing the Bottom of the Water Ripples

Drag the Rectangular Marquee Tool over the bottom of the water ripples to make a selection, as shown here.

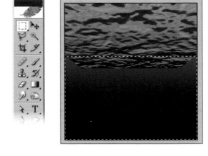

STEP 8. Blurring the Bottom of the Water Ripples

Choose Select > Feather from the menu at the top and set the Feather Radius to 60. The edges of the selection will blur by 60 pixels. Press Del to softly delete the bottom of the water, and then press Ctrl+D to deselect the selection.

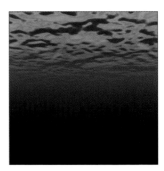

STEP 9. Shining Water Ripples

Press Ctrl+J to make another copy of the selected layer. In the Layers Palette, set the Blend Mode of the copied layer to Screen and the Fill to 100%. This will create the effect of the sun's rays hitting the surface of the water. However, this area is too wide.

STEP 10. Choosing the Lit Area

Choose the Elliptical Marquee Tool from the toolbox.

Go to the option bar and set the Feather value to 100 px. Click the tool on the top-right part of the image (which will be the center of where the sun's rays hit), and then hold down the Alt key and drag down to the lower-left side to create a selection frame that gets gradually bigger with respect to the top, as shown here.

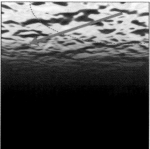

STEP 11. Deleting the Other Areas

Press Shift+Ctrl+I to invert the selection frame, press Del, and then press Ctrl+D to deselect the selection. The water gradually will fade due to the sun's rays that hit the upper-right corner.

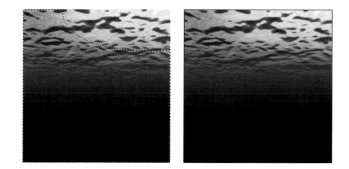

STEP 12. Making the Sun's Rays

Press Ctrl+J to make another copy of the selected layer. You can see this new layer (Layer 1 copy 2) in the Layers Palette.

Choose Filter > Blur > Motion Blur from the menu at the top, set the Angle to 90 and the Distance to 999 pixels, and then click on OK. Set the Blend Mode to Screen and the Fill to 100%. The selected image will drape downward to create the sun's rays, but the effect is too weak.

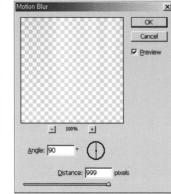
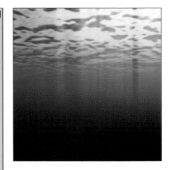

STEP 13. Creating a Black Background for the Sun's Rays

Click on the Create a New Layer button at the bottom of the Layers Palette to create a new layer, and then drag it right below the sun ray layer (Layer 1 copy 2). Press Ctrl+Del to fill in the new layer with the background color (black). In the Layers Palette, click on the Linked Layer icon in front of the sun ray layer (Layer 1 copy 2) to link this layer to the Layer 2 layer. Then, press Ctrl+E to merge (Link Merged) the linked layers.

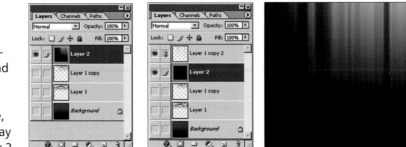

STEP 14. Sharpening the Sun's Rays Image

Choose Image > Adjustments > Curves and shape the curve into an S. Then, click on OK. This will make the sun's rays sharper and brighter.

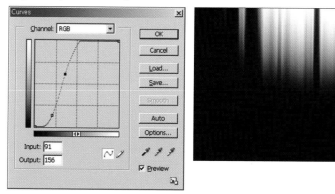

STEP 16. Brightening the Sun's Rays

Choose Image > Adjustments > Curves from the menu at the top, shape the curve to make the sun's rays brighter, and then click on OK.

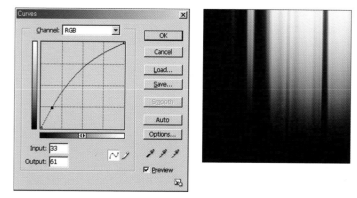

STEP 15. Making the Sun's Rays Longer

Choose Filter > Blur > Motion Blur from the menu at the top, set the Angle to 90 and the Distance to 680 pixels, and then click on OK. This will make the sun's rays longer.

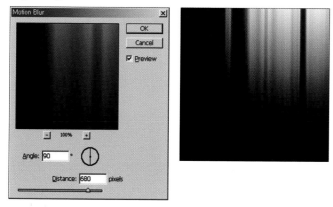

STEP 17. Blending the Sun's Rays

In the Layers Palette, set the Blend Mode of the sun ray layer to Screen. This will blend the bright sun's rays with the water.

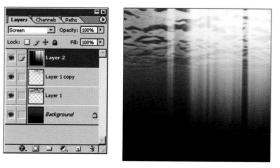

STEP 18. Creating 3D Sun Rays

Press Ctrl+T to apply the Free Transform command. Drag on the handles around the image while you hold down the Ctrl key to make the sun's rays fan out from the top-right corner, as shown here, and then press Enter.

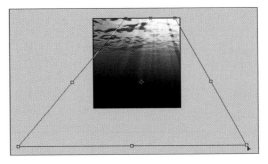

STEP 19. Setting Up the Brush

Click on the Foreground Color button and set it to white. Then, choose the Brush Tool.

Right-click on the work window to open the Brush Preset panel. Choose a basic brush shape from the list, as shown here, and set the size to 600 px.

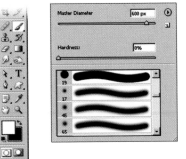

STEP 20. Lighting Up the Top-Right Part of the Image

Click on the Create a New Layer button at the bottom of the Layers Palette to create a new layer.

Then, click on the top-right part of the image. The large, soft brush that you set up in the previous step will be applied to create what looks like white light.

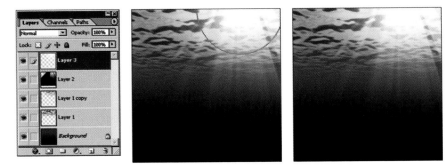

STEP 21. Cutting Out the Necessary Areas

Select the Crop tool from the toolbox. Drag the Crop Tool over the part of the image that you need and press Enter to crop the image.

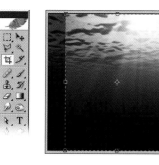

STEP 22. Entering the Title

Use the Horizontal Type Tool from the tool-box to type in the title.

Then, adjust the font and font size in the Character Palette. Large, white text entered on the black background will appear too harsh; therefore, you should adjust the Fill to make the effect softer.

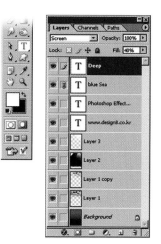

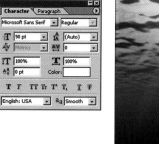

Effect 8: Soft Sky

You will use various filters to create a sky filled with clouds. You will use rather simple methods to create what looks like an actual photograph of a real sky. As you've seen before, every time the Cloud filter is applied, you get a different shape. You can take advantage of this feature to create the image.

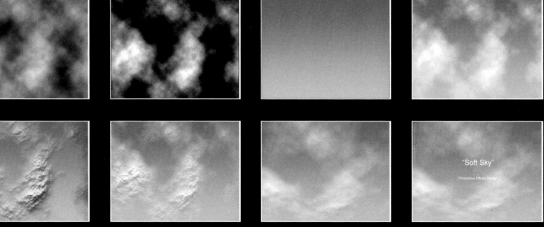

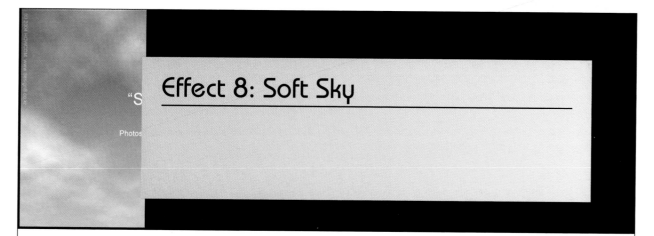

Effect 8: Soft Sky

Total Steps

STEP 1.   Creating a New Work Window
STEP 2.   Making Clouds
STEP 3.   Sharpening the Clouds
STEP 4.   Making the Sky Background
STEP 5.   Making Cloud-Shaped Selections
STEP 6.   Making Clouds
STEP 7.   Making Black Cloud Channels

STEP 8.   Making 3D Clouds
STEP 9.   Deleting in the Shape of the Clouds
STEP 10.   Blending the Dark Areas
STEP 11.   Softening the Darker Areas
STEP 12.   Making 3D Clouds
STEP 13.   Entering the Title

STEP 1. Creating a New Work Window

Press Ctrl+N to create a new work window. Click on the Preset box and choose 640×480 to create a 640×480-pixel workspace, and then click on OK.

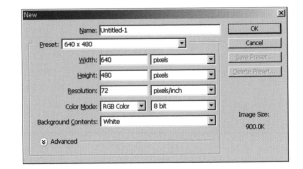

STEP 2. Making Clouds

Make sure your background is set to white. Press Ctrl+J to add a new layer. Choose Filter > Render > Clouds from the menu at the top to create irregular black and white clouds. Press Ctrl+F to apply the command again. Every time the command is repeated, a different cloud shape will be created. Continue repeating the command until you arrive at the shape you want.

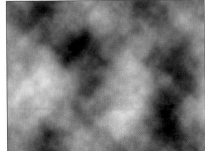

STEP 3. Sharpening the Clouds

Choose Image > Adjustments > Levels from the menu at the top. Set the Input Levels to 84, 1.00, and 213, and then click on OK.

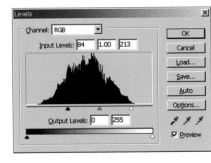

STEP 4. Making the Sky Background

Choose the Background layer from the Layers Palette and click on the Layer Visibility icon of the cloud layer right above it to hide the layer from view.

In the toolbox, set the foreground color to blue (RGB=69, 105, 178) and the background color to sky blue (RGB=147, 212, 245).

Choose the Gradient Tool from the toolbox, click on the top of the work window, and drag downward to create the sky blue gradient shown here.

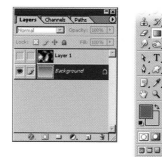

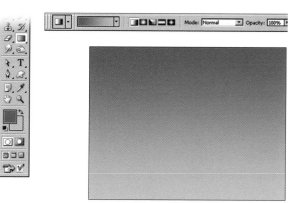

STEP 5. Making Cloud-Shaped Selections

Click on the hidden cloud layer in the Layers Palette so that it is visible again.

Then, click on the Channels Palette to open it. Click on the RGB channel while you are holding down the Ctrl key to create a selection frame of the bright areas of the image.

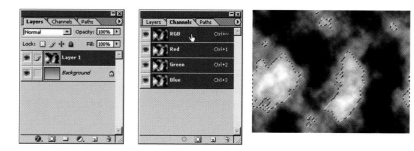

STEP 6. Making Clouds

In the toolbox, click on the Default Background and Foreground Colors button to set the foreground color to black and the background color to white.

Click on the Layers Palette to open it. Click on the Create a New Layer button at the bottom of the Layers Palette to create a new layer. Press Ctrl+Del to fill in the new layer with the background color (white). In the Layers Palette, click on the Layer Visibility icon in front of the black cloud layer (Layer 1) to hide it from view. Press Ctrl+D to deselect the selection, and then check your results. You will see that white clouds have been created on the sky blue background. The bottom of the clouds should be darker because there is no sun here.

STEP 7. Making Black Cloud Channels

Click on the hidden cloud layer in the Layers Palette and click on the Layer Visibility icon of the white cloud layer on top of it to hide it from view.

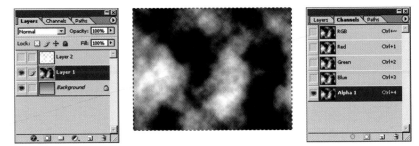

Choose the Rectangular Marquee Tool from the toolbox and select the entire cloud image in Layer 1.

Press Ctrl+C to make a copy of the layer. Click on the Channels Palette to open it, and then click on the Create New Channel button in the Channels Palette to make a new alpha channel (Alpha 1). Press Ctrl+V to paste the copied black cloud layer into the new alpha channel. Press Ctrl+D to deselect the selection.

STEP 8. Making 3D Clouds

Click on the Layers Palette to open it. Click on the Create a New Layer button at the bottom of the Layers Palette to create a new layer. Press Ctrl+Del to fill in the new layer with the background color (white).

Choose Filter > Render > Lighting Effects from the menu at the top, set the Texture Channel to Alpha 1 to create a 3D effect, and adjust the source of the light so it originates from the upper-left corner. Click on OK to accept the changes in the Lighting Effects dialog box. This will create 3D clouds on the white image.

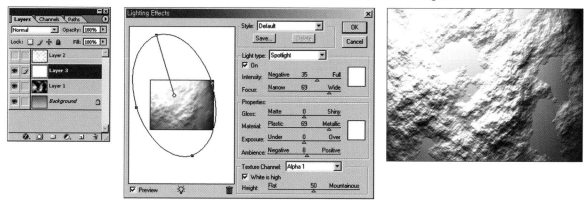

STEP 9. Deleting in the Shape of the Clouds

In the Layers Palette, click on the white cloud layer while you hold down the Ctrl key to make a selection frame of the clouds. Press Shift+Ctrl+I to invert the selection frames, and then press Del to delete everything but the clouds. In the Layers Palette, click on the Layer Visibility icon in front of the white cloud layer (Layer 1) to hide it from view, and then check your results. Press Ctrl+D to deselect the selection.

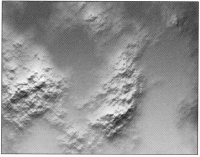

STEP 10. Blending the Dark Areas

Drag the 3D cloud layer to the very top of the Layers Palette, and then set the Blend Mode to Multiply and the Fill to 50%. Click on the Layer Visibility icon of the white cloud layer below it to make the layer visible again. The 3D effect will be applied to the white clouds, but the darker areas of the image are too rugged.

STEP 11. Softening the Darker Areas

Choose Filter > Blur > Gaussian Blur from the menu at the top, set the Radius to 10 pixels, and then click on OK. This will soften the darker areas of the clouds to make them appear more realistic.

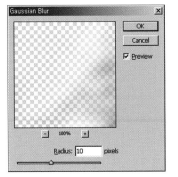

STEP 12. Making 3D Clouds

In the Layers Palette, click on the Linked Layer icon in front of the white cloud layer to link the two cloud layers. Press Ctrl+E to merge the layers.

Press Ctrl+T to apply the Free Transform command, drag out the handles around the image while holding down the Ctrl key to create a strong 3D effect, and then press Enter to apply the transformation. If you run out of room, press Ctrl+− to make the image smaller or drag on the edges of the work window to make the gray space larger.

STEP 13. Entering the Title

Use the Horizontal Type Tool from the toolbox to type in the title.

Then, adjust the font and font size in the Character Palette. Select white as the foreground color. Change the fill in the Layers Palette to lighten the white text.

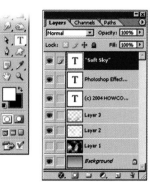

Effect 9: Woodcut Style Photograph

You can learn how to make a dark photograph appear as if it has been carved on wood. In this project, you will complete a series of simple steps to achieve the woodcut effect for a truly spectacular poster. By making the color of the person in the image different from the color of the background image, you can emphasize the person in the photograph.

Woodcut Style Photograph

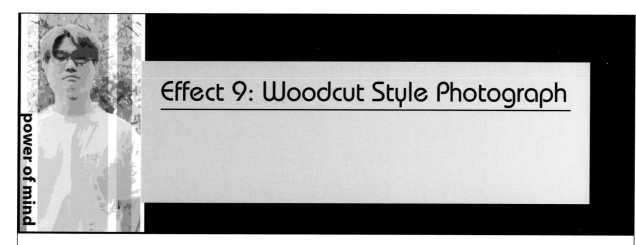

Total Steps

STEP 1.   Correcting the Source Photo's Brightness

STEP 2.   Adding Cutout Effects to the Image

STEP 3.   Strengthening the Image Color

STEP 4.   Copying the Subject to a New Layer

STEP 5.   Changing the Subject's Color

STEP 6.   Blending the Original Image

STEP 7.   Adding and Blending White Vertical Strips

STEP 8.   Adding a Solid White Strip

STEP 9.   Adding Text to Complete the Image

STEP 10. Performing the Final Step

STEP 1. Correcting the Source Photo's Brightness

From the File menu, select Open and open the Book\Sources\Woodcut Raw Image (man).jpg file from the supplementary CD-ROM.

Choose Image > Adjustments > Levels to open the Levels dialog box.

Drag the middle Input Levels slider to the left, and then click on OK to brighten the image.

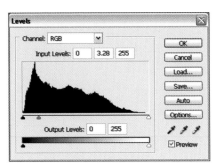

STEP 2. Adding Cutout Effects to the Image

Copy the Background layer by dragging it onto the Create a New Layer button on the Layers Palette.

With the new Background copy layer selected in the Layers Palette, select Filter > Artistic > Cutout to open the Cutout dialog box. Adjust the dialog box settings as shown here, and then click on OK.

STEP 3. Strengthening the Image Color

With the Background copy layer still selected, choose Image > Adjustments > Hue/Saturation. Drag the sliders in the Hue/Saturation dialog box to the settings shown here, and then click on OK.

STEP 4. Copying the Subject to a New Layer

Choose the Polygonal Lasso Tool from the toolbox, and then select the man in the image, as shown here. Press Ctrl+C to copy the selection, and then press Ctrl+V to paste the selection into a new layer named Layer 1.

STEP 5. Changing the Subject's Color

With the Layer 1 layer still selected in the Layers Palette, select Image > Adjustments > Hue/Saturation from the menu bar.

Drag the sliders in the Hue/Saturation dialog box to the settings shown here, and then click on OK. This will give your subject an orange hue.

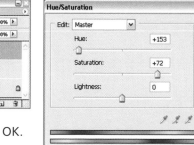

STEP 6. Blending the Original Image

Copy the Background layer by dragging it onto the Create a New Layer button on the Layers Palette. Drag the new Background copy 2 layer to the top of the Layers Palette.

With the Background copy 2 layer still selected in the Layers Palette, click on the Add a Layer Style button, and then click on Blending Options. Choose Overlay from the Blend Mode drop-down list in the Layer Style dialog box, and then click on OK to mix layer colors evenly.

STEP 7. Adding and Blending White Vertical Strips

Click on the Create a New Layer button on the Layers Palette to add a new layer named Layer 2.

Choose the Rectangular Marquee Tool from the toolbox, and select the three areas shown here in white. (After you select the first area, press and hold the Shift key as you make the other two selections.)

Using the Color palette, set the foreground color to white (RGB=255, 255, 255).

Use the Paint Bucket Tool or press Alt+Del to fill the selection marquee with the white foreground color.

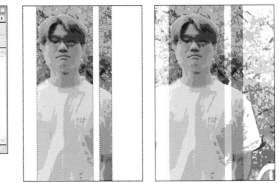

Choose Select, Deselect to remove the selection marquee. With the Layer 2 layer still selected in the Layers Palette, click on the Add a Layer Style button, and then click on Blending Options. Choose Overlay from the Blend Mode drop-down list in the Layer Style dialog box, and then click on OK to mix layer colors evenly.

STEP 8. Adding a Solid White Strip

Click on the Create a New Layer button on the Layers Palette to make a new layer named Layer 3.

Choose the Rectangular Marquee Tool from the toolbox, and select the two areas shown here in white. (After you select the first area, press and hold the Shift key as you make the other selection.)

With white still specified as the foreground color, use the Paint Bucket Tool or press Alt+Del to fill the selection marquee with white. Choose Select > Deselect to remove the selection marquee.

STEP 9. Adding Text to Complete the Image

Click on the Default Foreground and Background Colors button in the toolbox to make the foreground color black and the background color white.

Choose the Horizontal Type Tool from the toolbox, and then open the Character Palette. Adjust the palette settings as shown here, click on the image, type CULTURE INC, and then click on the Commit Any Current Edits button on the Options bar.

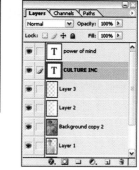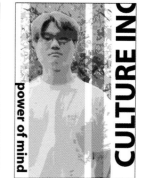

With the new CULTURE INC layer selected in the Layers Palette, choose Edit > Free Transform from the menu bar and use the handles that appear to rotate, size, and position the text, as shown here. Press Enter to finish the transformation.

Use the Horizontal Type tool and the Edit > Free Transform command to add and position the "power of mind" text at the left, as shown here. Press Enter to finish the transformation.

STEP 10. Performing the Final Step

Click on the CULTURE INC layer in the Layers Palette, and then click on the Create a New Layer button to make a new layer named Layer 4.

Press and hold the Ctrl button and click on the Layer 3 layer to make a selection on Layer 4 in the shape of the strips on Layer 3.

Choose the Rectangular Marquee Tool from the toolbox, and press and hold the Alt key while you drag over the right rectangle of the selection marquee to eliminate the right strip from the selection.

Choose the Gradient Tool from the toolbox, and then drag from the bottom of the left selection to the center to apply the gradient.

Choose Select > Deselect to remove the selection marquee.

With Layer 4 still selected in the Layers palette, use the Fill slider to change the Fill setting for Layer 4 to 26%.

Deepest Hole

Photoshop Effects Design

(c) 2004 HOWCOM All Right Reserved
www.design8.co.kr

Effect 10: Deepest Hole

The image of this very deep hole leads you to imagine that it might lead to a cave of treasures. This effect was made using a very basic filter, but as you can see, you can use this filter to create a very unique and sophisticated image.

Deepest Hole

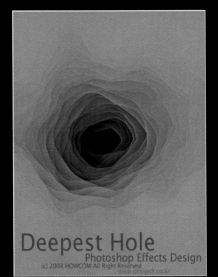

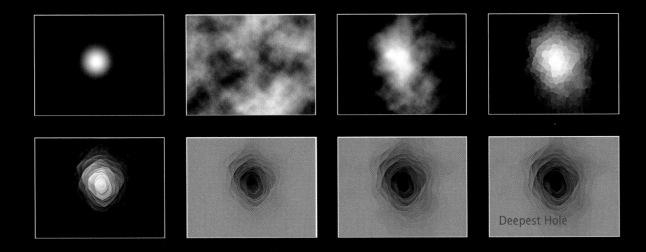

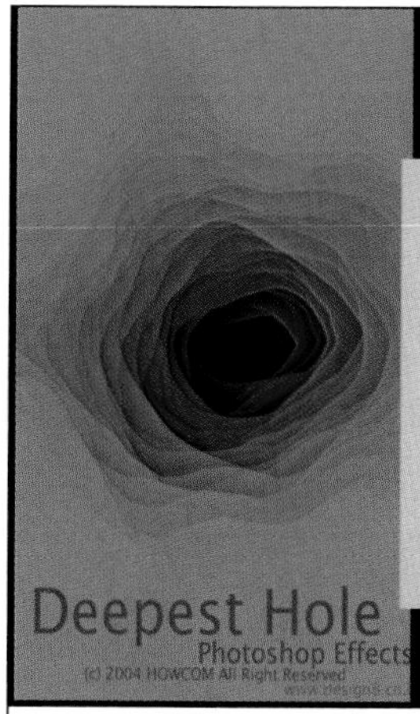

Effect 10: Deepest Hole

Deepest Hole
Photoshop Effects
(c) 2004 HOWCOM All Right Reserved
www.designii.c...

Total Steps

STEP 1.   Creating a New Work Window

STEP 2.   Setting Up the Brush

STEP 3.   Applying the Brush

STEP 4.   Making the Circle Bigger

STEP 5.   Making the Cloud Layer

STEP 6.   Blending the Cloud Image

STEP 7.   Creating Particles

STEP 8.   Blending Similar Colors

STEP 9.   Adding Dimensionality

STEP 10.   Emphasizing the Edges of the Image

STEP 11.   Blending the Two Layers

STEP 12.   Coloring the Black and White Image

STEP 13.   Adjusting the Depth of the Hole

STEP 14.   Choosing the Brown Color Used in the Image

STEP 15.   Entering the Title

STEP 16.   Entering the Remaining Text

STEP 1. Creating a New Work Window

Press Ctrl+N to create a new work window. Click on the Preset box, choose 640×480 to create a 640×480-pixel workspace, and then click on OK.

STEP 2. Setting Up the Brush

Click on the Default Foreground and Background Colors button and then the Switch Foreground and Background Colors button to set the foreground color to white and the background color to black. Then, choose the Brush Tool from the toolbox.

Right-click on the work window to open the Brush Preset Panel, and then choose a basic 200-pixel brush from the list, as shown here.

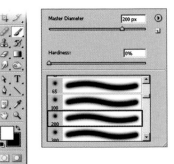

STEP 3. Applying the Brush

Press Ctrl+Del to fill in the entire image with the background color (black). Click on the Create a New Layer button at the bottom of the Layers Palette to create a new layer, and then click the Brush Tool on the middle of the image to create the soft dot shown here.

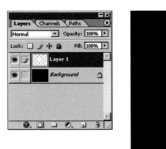

STEP 4. Making the Circle Bigger

Press Ctrl+T to apply the Free Transform command and drag out the handles around the image while holding down Shift+Alt to make the circle proportionately larger. Increase the circle until it fills up the entire workspace. Press Enter to accept the change.

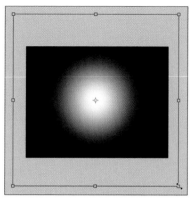 

STEP 5. Making the Cloud Layer

Click on the Create a New Layer button at the bottom of the Layers Palette to create a new layer, and then choose Filter > Render > Clouds from the menu at the top to create irregular black and white clouds. Press Ctrl+F to apply the command again. Every time the command is repeated, a different cloud shape will be created. Continue repeating the command until you arrive at the shape you want. You will get an image where the darker areas appear swirled together in the middle.

 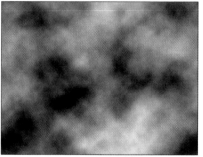

STEP 6. Blending the Cloud Image

In the Layers Palette, set the Blend Mode of the cloud layer to Linear Light and the Fill to 48%. The cloud image will cause the circle image to become irregular in shape.

Click on the Linked Layer icons on Layer 1 and Layer 2, select the Background layer, and then merge the layers.

STEP 7. Creating Particles

Choose Filter > Pixelate > Crystallize from the menu bar at the top, set the Cell Size to 30, and then click on OK. The image will now appear as an irregular 30-pixel crystal.

STEP 8. Blending Similar Colors

Choose Filter > Noise > Median from the menu bar at the top, set the Radius to 25 pixels, and then click on OK. The particles will clump together to create contour lines.

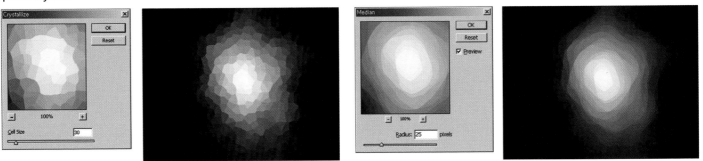

STEP 9. Adding Dimensionality

Press Ctrl+J to make a copy of the image layer, and then choose the Background layer from the bottom of the Layers Palette. Click on the Layer Visibility icon next to the copied layer to hide it.

Choose Filter > Render > Lighting Effects. Set up the graph on the left as shown here and set the Texture Channel to Red to create a 3D effect.

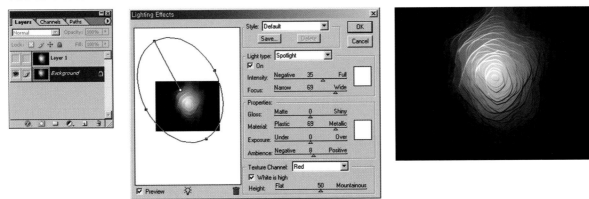

STEP 10. Emphasizing the Edges of the Image

Click on the hidden layer (Layer 1) in the Layers Palette to make it visible again.

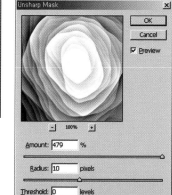

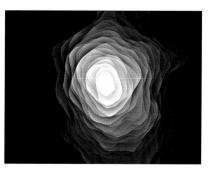

Then choose Filter > Sharpen > Unsharp Mask from the menu at the top and set the Amount to 479%, the Radius to 10 pixels, and the Threshold to 0 levels. Click on OK to accept the changes. This will emphasize the edges of the image to create a 3D effect.

STEP 11. Blending the Two Layers

In the Layers Palette, set the Blend Mode of the selected layer to Multiply and the Fill to 75%. The two images will be blended to create a realistic 3D effect.

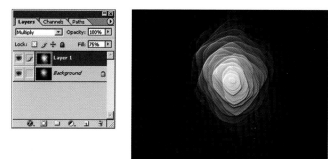

STEP 12. Coloring the Black and White Image

Click on the Create New Fill or Adjustment Layer button at the bottom of the Layers Palette and choose Gradient Map.

Click on the Gradient Color button in the middle of the panel to open the Gradient Editor Panel.

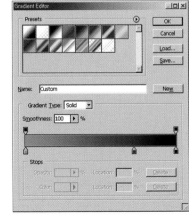

Click on the bottom of the gradient bar at the bottom of the panel to add a color tab and drag to move or double-click to set up the color. You can also drag the color tab out of the panel to delete the color. Set up the color tab as shown here—muddy yellow (RGB=167, 146, 84) > brown (RGB=83, 44, 27) > black. The image will take on a brownish tone to create a 3D hole. Click on OK to accept the changes.

STEP 13. Adjusting the Depth of the Hole

Choose the Background layer from the Layers Palette.

Choose Image > Adjustments > Curves from the menu at the top and shape the graph as shown here to create a deep, dark hole. Click on OK to accept the changes.

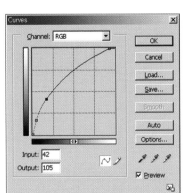
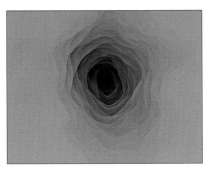

STEP 14. Choosing the Brown Color Used in the Image

Choose the Eyedropper Tool from the toolbox and click it on the inside of the hole to select the brown color of an appropriate brightness.

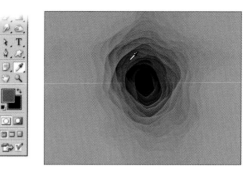

STEP 15. Entering the Title

Use the Horizontal Type Tool from the toolbox to type in the title.

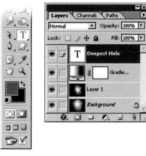

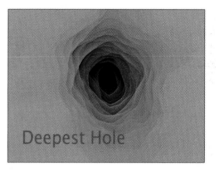

STEP 16. Entering the Remaining Text

Choose the Horizontal Type Tool from the toolbox and type in the remaining text. Link the text together and rotate it 90 degrees by choosing Edit > Transform > Rotate 90 CW.

Effect 11: Skyscraper City

In this effect, skyscrapers threaten to pierce the skies of a dark city.

Skyscraper City

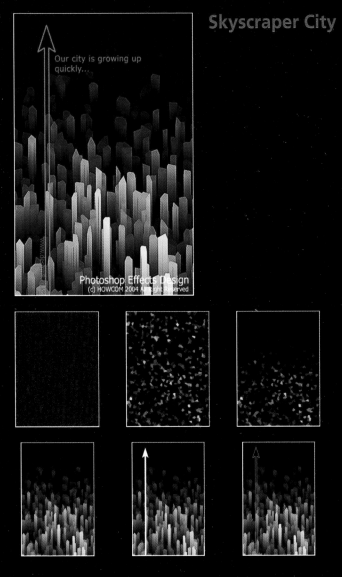

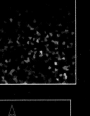
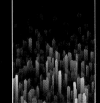
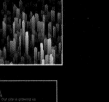

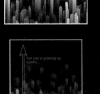

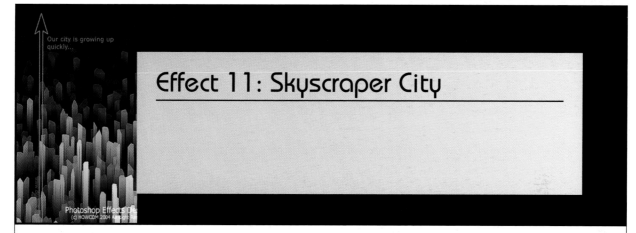

Effect 11: Skyscraper City

Total Steps

STEP 1.   Creating a New Work Window

STEP 2.   Applying Noise

STEP 3.   Making the Dots Larger

STEP 4.   Setting Up the Gradient

STEP 5.   Making the Top of the Image Dark

STEP 6.   Applying a Wind Effect to the Image

STEP 7.   Rotating the Image to Create Vertical Skyscrapers

STEP 8.   Emphasizing the Edges of the Image

STEP 9.   Blending Filter Effects

STEP 10. Coloring the Image

STEP 11. Cutting Out the Necessary Areas

STEP 12. Formatting the Line Tool as an Arrow

STEP 13. Drawing the Arrow

STEP 14. Modifying the Arrow Style

STEP 15. Entering Text

STEP 16. Entering the Remaining Text

STEP 1. Creating a New Work Window

Press Ctrl+N to create a new work window. Click on the Preset box and choose 640×480 to create a 640×480-pixel workspace. Choose Image > Rotate Canvas > 90 CW from the menu at the top to rotate the workspace 90 degrees clockwise so it is vertical.

In the toolbox, click on the Default Foreground and Background Colors button to set up the default colors. Set the foreground color to black and the background color to white, and then press Alt+Del to fill in the entire image with the foreground color (black).

STEP 2. Applying Noise

Choose Filter > Noise > Add Noise from the menu at the top and set the Amount to 29% and the Distribution to Gaussian. Then, check Monochromatic. This will create black and white noise over the entire image.

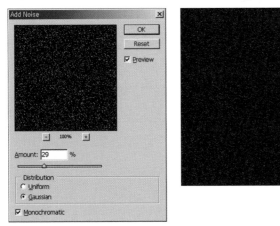

STEP 3. Making the Dots Larger

Choose Filter > Pixelate > Crystallize from the menu at the top and set the Cell Size to 20. This will make the particles small (20 pixels) and irregular.

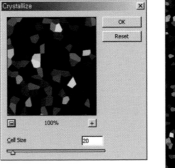

STEP 4. Setting Up the Gradient

Choose the Gradient Tool from the toolbox.

Then, open the Gradient Preset Panel and choose the second gradient (Foreground to Transparent).

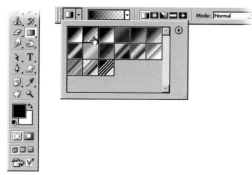

STEP 5. Making the Top of the Image Dark

Click on the Create a New Layer button at the bottom of the Layers Palette to create a new layer.

Then, click on the top edge of the image and drag it over to the middle. Press Ctrl+E to merge the two layers.

STEP 6. Applying a Wind Effect to the Image

Choose Image > Rotate Canvas > 90 CW to rotate the workspace 90 degrees clockwise. Choose Filter > Stylize > Wind from the menu at the top and set the Method to Wind and the Direction to From the Right.

This will make the particles appear to fly into the image. Press Ctrl+F six or seven times to repeat the application of the Wind filter to create the elongated effect shown here.

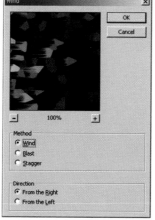
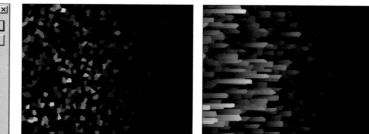

STEP 7. Rotating the Image to Create Vertical Skyscrapers

Choose Image > Rotate Canvas > 90 CCW to return the image back to its original position. You will now have what looks like many skyscrapers overlapping one another.

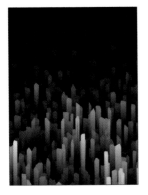

STEP 8. Emphasizing the Edges of the Image

Choose Filter > Sharpen > Unsharp Mask from the menu at the top and set the Amount to 500%, the Radius to 1.3 pixels, and the Threshold to 0 levels. This will make the edges of the image sharper and brighter.

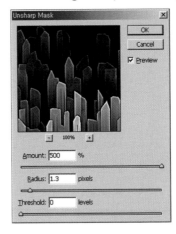 

STEP 9. Blending Filter Effects

After applying the filter, choose Edit > Fade Unsharp Mask from the menu at the top and set the Mode to Screen and the Opacity to 80% to make the effect more natural.

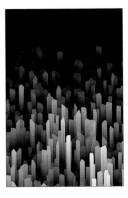

STEP 10. Coloring the Image

Click on the Create New Fill or Adjustment Layer button at the bottom of the Layers Palette and choose Gradient Map.

Click on the gradient in the middle of the Gradient Map dialog box to open the Gradient Editor.

Click on the bottom of the gradient bar at the bottom of the Gradient Editor to add a color tab, and drag to move or double-click to set up the color. You can also drag the color tab out of the panel to delete the color. Set up the color tab as shown here—black > dark brown (RGB=55, 0, 0) > brown (RGB=134, 65, 41) > yellow (RGB=242, 222, 85) > flesh (RGB=255, 255, 214). The black and white image will become brownish in tone.

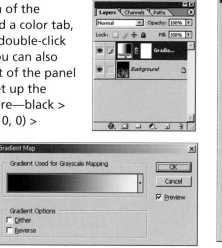

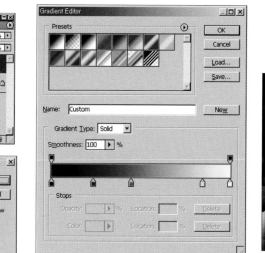

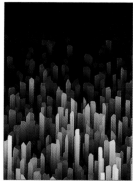

STEP 11. Cutting Out the Necessary Areas

Drag the Crop Tool over the part of the image that you need and press Enter to crop the image.

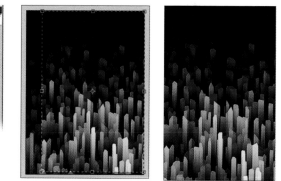

STEP 12. Formatting the Line Tool as an Arrow

In the toolbox, set the foreground color to white, and then choose the Line Tool.

In the option bar at the top, set the Weight to 8 px, and then click on the Geometry Options button (to the right of the Custom Shape Tool). In the resulting Arrowheads pane, set the options as shown in the figure.

STEP 13. Drawing the Arrow

Click on the bottom-left corner of the work window and drag to the top to draw in a white arrow, as shown here. Press Shift while you are drawing the arrow to make it perfectly vertical. Use the Move Tool to position the arrow.

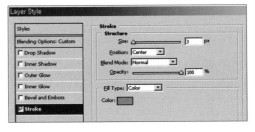

STEP 14. Modifying the Arrow Style

In the Layers Palette, set the Fill of the arrow layer to 0 to make it transparent, and then click on the Add a Layer Style button at the bottom.

Choose Stroke to open the Layer Style Panel, and then set the Size to 3 px, the Position to Center, and the Color to red. The arrow will be outlined in red.

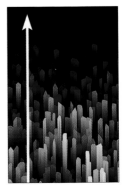
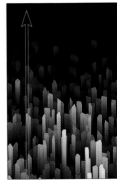

STEP 15. Entering Text

Create a new layer and click on the Foreground Color to set it to red. Use the Horizontal Type Tool from the toolbox to type in the title.

Then, adjust the font and font size in the Character Palette. Hold down the Ctrl key and drag the text to position it anywhere you want.

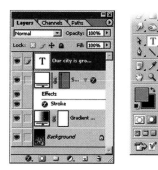  

STEP 16. Entering the Remaining Text

Use the Horizontal Type Tool from the toolbox to type in the remaining text. Make the arrows and some of the text stand out by making it red, and make the remaining text white.

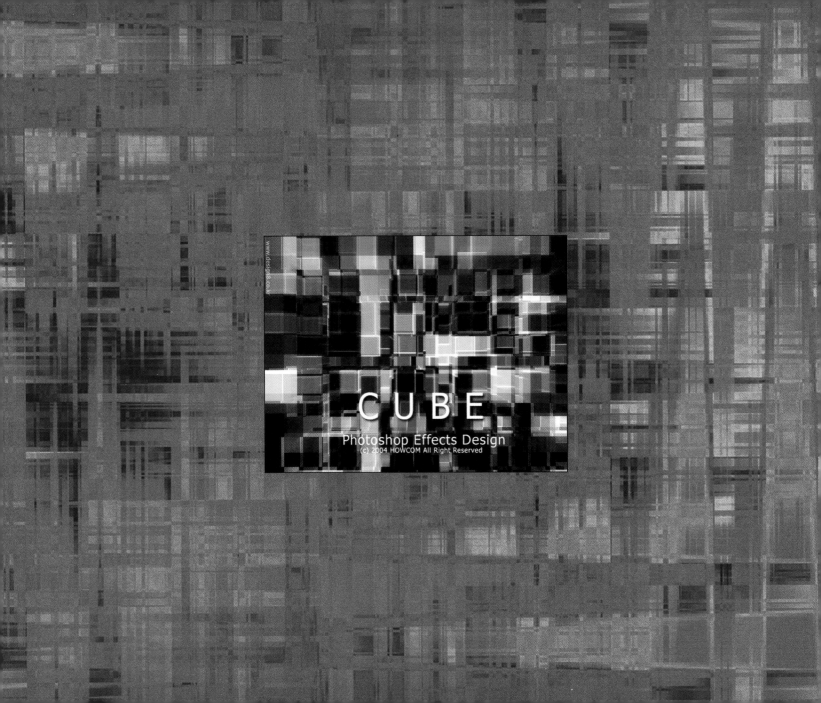

CUBE

Photoshop Effects Design

Effect 12: The Light Cube

In this example, light will be refracted and reflected through a lattice of brown and blue panes of glass. This will make a great poster for a film.

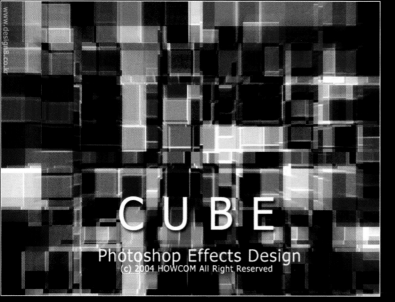

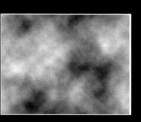 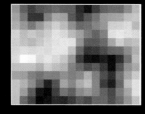 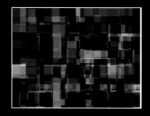 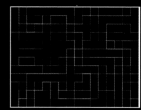

 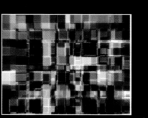 

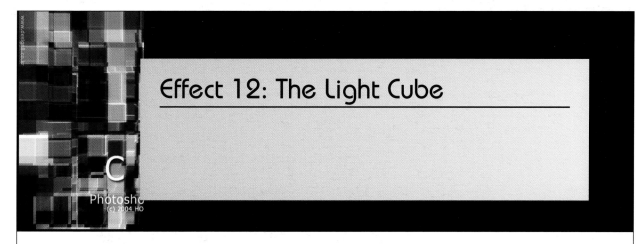

Effect 12: The Light Cube

Total Steps

STEP 1. Creating a New Work Window

STEP 2. Making Black and White Clouds

STEP 3. Sharpening the Clouds

STEP 4. Creating a Mosaic

STEP 5. Coloring the Black and White Image

STEP 6. Mixing the Mosaic

STEP 7. Blending the Filter Effect

STEP 8. Creating Mosaic Edges

STEP 9. Adjusting the Brightness of the Lines

STEP 10. Mixing the Edges

STEP 11. Blending the Edges

STEP 12. Making the Light Stronger

STEP 13. Sharpening the Cubic Image

STEP 14. Adjusting the Brightness of the Image

STEP 15. Creating a Reflection

STEP 16. Entering the Title

STEP 1. Creating a New Work Window

Press Ctrl+N to create a new work window. Click on the Preset box, choose 640×480 to create a 640×480-pixel workspace, and then click on OK.

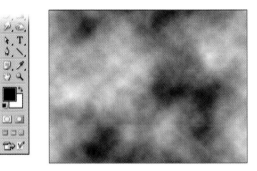

STEP 2. Making Black and White Clouds

In the toolbox, click on the Default Foreground and Background Colors button to set up the default color. Set the foreground color to black and the background color to white. Choose Filter > Render > Clouds from the menu at the top to create irregular black and white clouds. Press Ctrl+F to apply the command again. Every time the command is repeated, a different cloud shape will be created. Continue repeating the command until you arrive at the shape you like.

STEP 3. Sharpening the Clouds

Choose Image > Adjustments > Levels from the menu at the top, drag the black and white tabs below the graph to their starting positions as shown here to sharpen the clouds, and then click on OK to accept the changes.

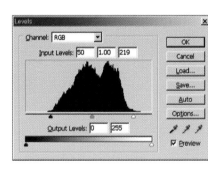

STEP 4. Creating a Mosaic

Choose Filter > Pixelate > Mosaic from the menu at the top, set the Cell Size to 40 square, and then click on OK. This will convert the clouds into a rectangular mosaic.

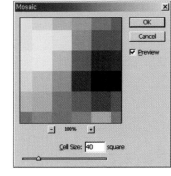

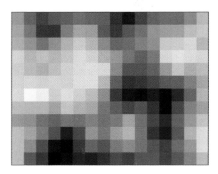

STEP 5. Coloring the Black and White Image

Choose Image > Adjustments > Hue/Saturation from the menu at the top; check Colorize; set the Hue to 190, the Saturation to 40, and the Lightness to 4; and then click on OK. This will change the black and white image to a bluish (cyan) tone.

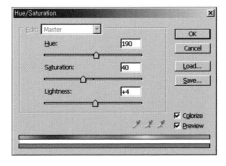

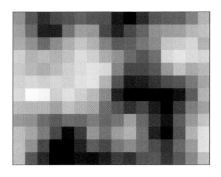

STEP 6. Mixing the Mosaic

Press Ctrl+J to make a copy of the image layer and then choose the Background layer from the bottom of the Layers Palette. Click on the Layer Visibility icon next to the copied layer to hide it.

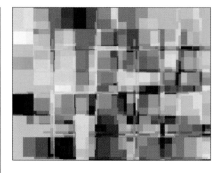

Then, choose Filter > Distort > Wave from the menu at the top, set the Type to Square, the Number of Generators to 5, the Wavelength to 132/393, the Amplitude to 1/71, and the Scale to 100%/100%. This will randomly mix up the mosaic image. Click on OK.

STEP 7. Blending the Filter Effect

After you apply the Wave filter, choose Edit > Fade Wave from the menu at the top, set the Mode to Difference, and then click on OK. The color will be inverted so the original mosaic and the filter image overlap to make some of the squares brown and the others blue.

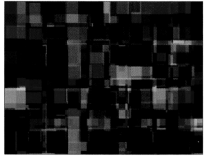

STEP 8. Mosaic Edges

Click on the hidden layer (Layer 1) in the Layers Palette to make it visible again.

Then, choose Filter > Stylize > Find Edges from the menu at the top. The edges of the mosaic will appear on top of the white background. Press Ctrl+I to invert the image colors so that the mosaic edges will show up on a black background.

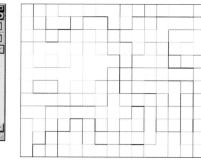

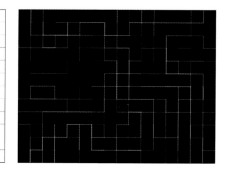

STEP 9. Adjusting the Brightness of the Lines

Choose Image > Adjustments > Levels from the menu at the top, drag the white tab of the histogram to the left as shown here to brighten the mosaic edges, and then click on OK.

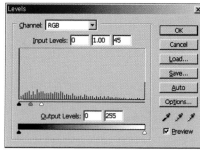

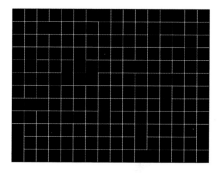

STEP 10. Mixing the Edges

Choose Filter > Distort > Wave and apply the effect using the same settings as before. The mosaic edges will mix together randomly.

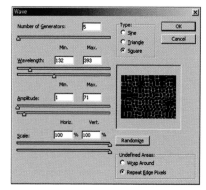

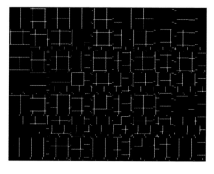

STEP 11. Blending the Edges

In the Layers Palette, set the Blend Mode of the edge layer (Layer 1) to Color Dodge and the Fill to 30%. This will create gaps of light between the cubic images.

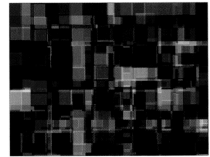

STEP 12. Making the Light Stronger

Press Ctrl+J to make a copy of the selected layer, and then, in the Layers Palette, set the Blend Mode of the copied layer to Linear Dodge and the Fill to 40%.

Choose Filter > Blur > Radial Blur from the menu at the top and set the Amount to 27, the Blur Method to Zoom, and the Quality to Good. This will make the gaps of light between the cubic images appear to shine. Click on OK to accept the changes.

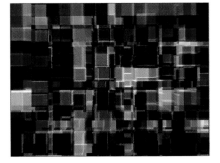

STEP 13. Sharpening the Cubic Image

In the Layers Palette, drag and drop the Background layer onto the Create a New Layer button to make a copy of the layer and set the Blend Mode to Linear Light and the Fill to 20%. The cubic image may appear sharper, but the overall image has become too dark.

STEP 14. Adjusting the Brightness of the Image

Choose Image > Adjustments > Levels from the menu at the top, move the white and black tabs below the histogram to the right as shown here to brighten the overall image, and then click on OK.

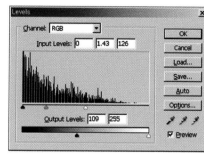

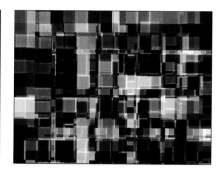

STEP 15. Creating a Reflection

Choose Filter > Blur > Radial Blur from the menu at the top; set the Amount to 27, the Blur Method to Zoom, and the Quality to Best; and then click on OK. The blended cubic image will transform with respect to the amount of light to create the effect of a reflection.

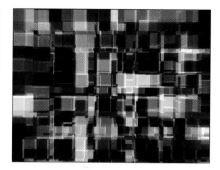

STEP 16. Entering the Title

Use the Horizontal Type Tool from the toolbox to type in the title.

Then, adjust the font and font size in the Character Palette.

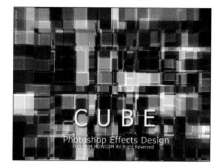

Effect 13: Creative Artwork

In this project, you will take an old portrait and transform it into a work of art. You will emphasize the details in the picture effectively and apply color to the darker regions. You will overlap and blend textures made or taken from picture sources to complete this homage to the man who set himself on fire in the name of independence.

Creative Artwork

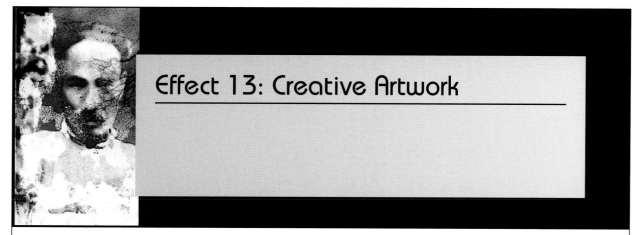

Effect 13: Creative Artwork

Total Steps

STEP 1. Resizing the Source Photo
STEP 2. Copying the Layer and Removing Noise
STEP 3. Lightening the Image
STEP 4. Copying a Layer and Emphasizing the Tones
STEP 5. Adjusting Image Brightness
STEP 6. Blending the Background Copy 2 Layer
STEP 7. Copying and Smudging a Layer
STEP 8. Blending the Smudged Layer
STEP 9. Colorizing the Background Copy 3 Layer
STEP 10. Colorizing the Background Copy 2 Layer
STEP 11. Colorizing the Background Copy Layer
STEP 12. Adding Black Borders
STEP 13. Adding Texture to the Black Borders
STEP 14. Blending the Black Borders
STEP 15. Adding White Borders
STEP 16. Adding Texture to the White Borders
STEP 17. Emphasizing the Black Borders
STEP 18. Adding a Cloud Texture Layer
STEP 19. Converting the Clouds to Ink Blots
STEP 20. Adjusting the Texture's Gray Tones

STEP 21. Inverting and Resizing the Texture
STEP 22. Blurring the Texture
STEP 23. Blending the Texture
STEP 24. Colorizing the Texture Layer
STEP 25. Choosing a Flower Brush
STEP 26. Making a Bouquet of Flowers on a New Layer
STEP 27. Blending the Bouquet
STEP 28. Importing the Tree Image
STEP 29. Arranging and Blending the Tree Image
STEP 30. Restoring the Color of the Background Copy Layer
STEP 31. Restoring the Color of the Background Copy 2 Layer
STEP 32. Restoring the Color of the Background Copy 3 Layer
STEP 33. Blending the Black Borders
STEP 34. Adjusting the Bouquet Color and Completing the Image

STEP 1. Resizing the Source Photo

Select File > Open and open the Book\Sources\Creative Artwork Raw Image (man).tif file from the supplementary CD-ROM. Due to the portrait's age, noise covers it and the overall size is very small.

Select Image > Image Size to open the Image Size dialog box. In the Pixel Dimensions area of the dialog box, enter 300 in the Width text box and choose Percent from the Width drop-down list. Make sure the Height settings also change to 300 percent, and then click on OK to increase the image's size by 300 percent.

Use the Navigator Palette to zoom the image to 25% so you can see the full image onscreen. Finally, select Image > Mode > RGB Color to change the image to RGB color mode, even though it still appears black and white.

STEP 2. Copying the Layer and Removing Noise

Copy the Background layer by dragging it onto the Create a New Layer button on the Layers Palette.

With the new Background copy layer selected, choose Filter > Noise > Median from the menu bar. Change the Radius to 17 in the Median dialog box, and then click on OK to remove the noise and simplify the image.

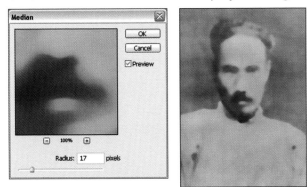

STEP 3. Lightening the Image

Select Image > Adjustments > Levels to open the Levels dialog box.

Drag the center Input Levels slider to the position shown here, and then click on OK to lighten the image overall.

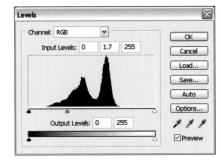

STEP 4. Copying a Layer and Emphasizing the Tones

Copy the Background layer by dragging it onto the Create a New Layer button on the Layers Palette. Drag the new Background copy 2 layer to the top of the Layers Palette.

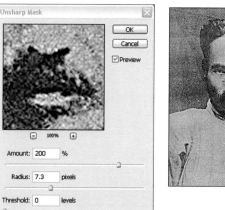

With the Background copy 2 layer still selected, select Filter > Sharpen > Unsharp Mask.

Choose the settings shown here in the Unsharp Mask dialog box, and then click on OK to emphasize the dark and light tones in the image.

STEP 5. Adjusting Image Brightness

Select Image > Adjustments > Curves. In the Curves dialog box, bend the curve into the shape shown here. To do so, click on the diagonal line to create points on the curve, and then drag them into position. Click on OK to apply the changes.

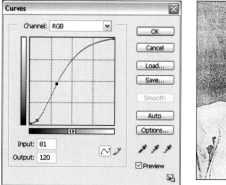

STEP 6. Blending the Background Copy 2 Layer

With the Background copy 2 layer still selected in the Layers Palette, click on the Add a Layer Style button, and then click on Blending Options.

Choose Darken from the Blend Mode drop-down list in the Layer Style dialog box, and then click on OK. Only the black pixels in the current layer will appear over the image from the layer below.

STEP 7. Copying and Smudging a Layer

Copy the Background layer by dragging it onto the Create a New Layer button on the Layers Palette. Drag the new Background copy 3 layer to the top of the Layers Palette.

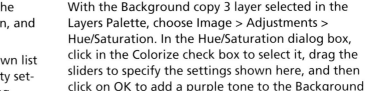

With the new layer still selected, select Filter > Artistic > Smudge Stick. Choose the settings shown here in the Smudge Stick dialog box, and then click on OK to set the configurations and make it appear as if the image were drawn by hand using a short piece of charcoal.

STEP 8. Blending the Smudged Layer

With the Background copy 3 layer still selected in the Layers Palette, click on the Add a Layer Style button, and then click on Blending Options.

Choose Linear Light from the Blend Mode drop-down list in the Layer Style dialog box, change the Fill Opacity setting to 33%, and then click on OK to create a strong blend between the layers.

STEP 9. Colorizing the Background Copy 3 Layer

With the Background copy 3 layer selected in the Layers Palette, choose Image > Adjustments > Hue/Saturation. In the Hue/Saturation dialog box, click in the Colorize check box to select it, drag the sliders to specify the settings shown here, and then click on OK to add a purple tone to the Background copy 3 layer.

STEP 10. Colorizing the Background Copy 2 Layer

Click on the Background copy 2 layer in the Layers Palette. Choose Image > Adjustments > Hue/Saturation. In the Hue/Saturation dialog box, click in the Colorize check box to select it, drag the sliders to specify the settings shown here, and then click on OK to add a blue tone to the Background copy 2 layer.

STEP 11. Colorizing the Background Copy Layer

Click on the Background copy layer in the Layers Palette. Choose Image > Adjustments > Hue/Saturation. In the Hue/Saturation dialog box, click in the Colorize check box to select it, drag the sliders to specify the settings shown here, and then click on OK to add a brown tone to the Background copy layer.

STEP 12. Adding Black Borders

Choose the Rectangular Marquee Tool from the toolbox and select the rectangular shapes shown here. (After you select the first area, press and hold the Shift key as you make additional selections.)

Click on the Create a New Layer button on the Layers Palette to add a new layer named Layer 1. Drag the new layer to the top of the Layers Palette. Click on the Default Foreground and Background Colors button on the toolbox to set the foreground color to black.

 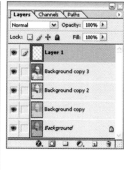 

Use the Paint Bucket Tool or press Alt+Del to fill the selection with black on Layer 1. Choose Select > Deselect to remove the selection marquee.

STEP 13. Adding Texture to the Black Borders

With the Layer 1 layer still selected in the Layers Palette, choose Filter > Distort > Displace. Set both Scale values to 30% in the Displace dialog box, and then click on OK.

In the Choose a Displacement Map dialog box that appears, select the Book\Sources\Creative Artwork Displacement Map.psd file from the supplementary CD-ROM, and then click on Open to use that file as the displace map. The borders will take on the rough appearance of chalk strokes.

STEP 14. Blending the Black Borders

With the Layer 1 layer still selected in the Layers Palette, click on the Add a Layer Style button, and then click on Blending Options.

Choose Soft Light from the Blend Mode drop-down list in the Layer Style dialog box, and then click on OK to blend the borders into the image.

STEP 15. Adding White Borders

Copy Layer 1 by dragging it onto the Create a New Layer button on the Layers Palette. Choose Layer > Layer Style > Clear Layer Style from the menu bar to remove the Soft Light blending style from the new Layer 1 copy layer.

With the new layer still selected, choose Image > Adjustments > Invert. The color on the layer will invert, making the black border white.

Select Edit > Free Transform, resize the borders as shown here, and then press Enter.

Select Filter > Distort > Displace. Set both Scale values to 30% in the Displace dialog box, click on Tile under Displacement Map, and then click on OK.

In the Choose a Displacement Map dialog box that appears, select the Book\Sources\Creative Artwork Displacement Map.psd file from the supplementary CD-ROM, and then click on Open to use that file as the displace map. The smaller white borders will take on an even rougher appearance.

STEP 16. Adding Texture to the White Borders

With the Layer 1 copy layer still selected in the Layers Palette, choose Filter > Render > Difference Clouds. A black and white texture will appear in the white border. Press Ctrl+F again as needed to reapply the Difference Clouds filter until the texture reaches the desired appearance.

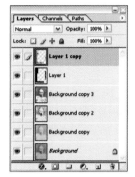

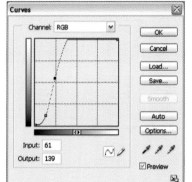

Select Image > Adjustments > Curves. In the Curves dialog box, bend the curve into the shape shown here. To do so, click the diagonal line to create points on the curve, and then drag them into position. Click on OK to apply the changes and emphasize the whites in the texture. Choose Edit > Transform > Rotate 180° to flip the white border.

With the Layer 1 copy layer still selected in the Layers Palette, click on the Add a Layer Style button, and then click on Blending Options. Choose Linear Dodge from the Blend Mode drop-down list in the Layer Style dialog box, change the Fill Opacity setting to 60%, and then click on OK to blend the borders into the image.

STEP 17. Emphasizing the Black Borders

Click on the Layer 1 layer in the Layers Palette. Open the Layer Style drop-down list in the upper-left corner of the Layers Palette, and then click on Color Burn to intensify the blurred black borders.

STEP 18. Adding a Cloud Texture Layer

Click on the Create a New Layer button on the Layers Palette to add a new layer named Layer 2. Drag the Layer 2 layer to the top of the Layers Palette, and then click on the Layer Visibility icon beside each of the other layers in the image to hide them all.

With the Layer 2 layer still selected, choose Filter > Render > Clouds from the menu bar to fill the layer with a black and white cloud texture.

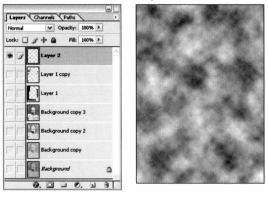

STEP 19. Converting the Clouds to Ink Blots

Choose Filter > Sketch > Plaster from the menu bar to open the Plaster dialog box. Choose the settings shown here, and then click on OK to make the black areas in the texture appear like raised inkblots.

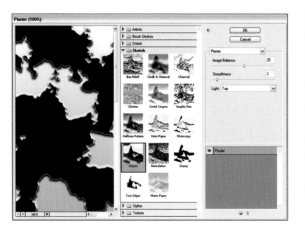

STEP 20. Adjusting the Texture's Gray Tones

With the Layer 2 layer still selected in the Layers Palette, choose Image > Adjustments > Curves. In the Curves dialog box, bend the curve into the shape shown here. To do so, click the diagonal line to create points on the curve, and then drag them into position. Click on OK to apply the changes and evenly distribute the gray background tones on the layer.

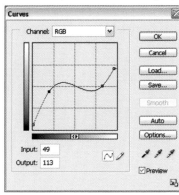 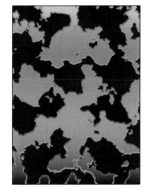

STEP 21. Inverting and Resizing the Texture

Select Image > Adjustments > Invert to invert the texture's color. Select Edit > Free Transform, drag the upper-right handle to reduce the texture image as shown here, and then press Enter to finish the transformation.

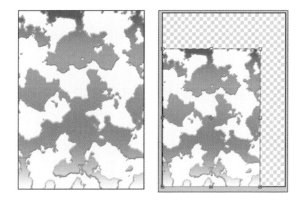

STEP 22. Blurring the Texture

With the Layer 2 layer still selected, click on the Add Layer Mask button on the Layers Palette to apply a mask to the layer. Click on the Switch Foreground and Background Colors button in the toolbox to set the foreground color to black and the background color to white.

Choose the Gradient tool, and then click on the Linear Gradient button on the Options bar. Drag from the upper-right corner of the reduced texture image to its center. The black areas of the gradient identify the transparent areas of the layer mask, creating graduated transparency in the texture.

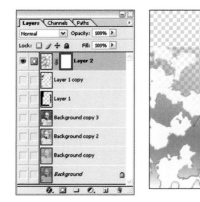

STEP 23. Blending the Texture

Click on the Layer Visibility icon box beside each hidden layer in the Layers Palette to view all the layers. With the Layer 2 layer still selected in the palette, open the Layer Style drop-down list in the upper-left corner of the Layers Palette. Click on Overlay to add the mottled texture to the image.

STEP 24. Colorizing the Texture Layer

In the Layers Palette, click on the Layer thumbnail for the Layer 2 layer to enable you to make changes to the layer contents (rather than the mask). Choose Image > Adjustments > Hue/Saturation to open the Hue/Saturation dialog box.

Click in the Colorize check box to select it, drag the sliders to specify the settings shown here, and then click on OK to add a yellow tint to the texture layer.

STEP 25. Choosing a Flower Brush

Choose the Brush Tool from the toolbox. Click on the down arrow on the Options bar to open the Brush Preset Picker, and then click on the palette menu button in the upper-right corner of the Brush Preset Picker. Click on Special Effect Brushes in the menu, and then click on OK to replace the default brushes in the picker with the special effect brushes. (Choose Reset Brushes from the palette menu at any later time to return to the default brushes.)

Click on the first brush in the palette (the Azalea brush) and drag the Master Diameter slider to set the brush size to 100 px. Click on the Click to Open the Brush Preset Picker button on the Options bar to close the preset picker.

STEP 26. Making a Bouquet of Flowers on a New Layer

Click on the Create a New Layer button on the Layers Palette to add a new layer named Layer 3. Click or drag in the lower-right corner of the image to add a bouquet of flowers. Choose Image > Adjustments > Hue/Saturation to open the Hue/Saturation dialog box.

Click in the Colorize check box to select it, drag the sliders to specify the settings shown here, and then click on OK to change the color of the flowers to yellow.

STEP 27. Blending the Bouquet

With the Layer 3 layer still selected in the Layers Palette, open the Layer Style drop-down list in the upper-left corner of the Layers Palette. Click on Screen to blend the flowers with other elements of the image.

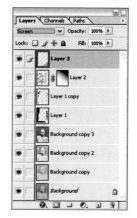

STEP 28. Importing the Tree Image

Select File > Open and open the Book\Sources\Creative Artwork Raw Image (tree).jpg file from the supplementary CD-ROM.

Choose the Move Tool from the toolbox, and then drag the tree image window to the image window for this project's file to place a copy of the tree on its own layer in the project file. Use the Move Tool to drag the tree on its layer (Layer 4) to the approximate position shown here.

STEP 29. Arranging and Blending the Tree Image

With Layer 4 still selected in the Layers Palette, choose Edit > Free Transform. Use the handles that appear to rotate the tree image 180°, drag it to the upper-right corner of the layer, and increase its size. Press Enter to finish the transformation.

Open the Layer Style drop-down list in the upper-left corner of the Layers Palette, and then click on Linear Burn. Also, use the Fill slider on the Layers Palette to change the Fill setting to 33% for Layer 4. Now, the white areas of the tree have become transparent, and the black regions blend into the image.

STEP 30. Restoring the Color of the Background Copy Layer

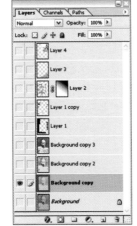

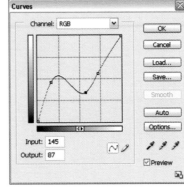

In the Layers Palette, right-click on the Layer Visibility icon beside the Background copy layer, and then click on Show/Hide for all the other layers in the menu so that only the Background copy layer is visible.

Click on the Background copy layer to select it, and then select Image > Adjustments > Curves. In the Curves dialog box, bend the curve into the shape shown here. To do so, click the diagonal line to create points on the curve, and then drag them into position. Click on OK to apply the changes and strengthen the layer's colors.

STEP 31. Restoring the Color of the Background Copy 2 Layer

Click on the Background copy 2 layer in the Layers Palette to both redisplay and select the layer.

Choose Image > Adjustments > Hue/Saturation and enter the values shown here.

Click on the Background copy 3 layer in the Layers Palette to both redisplay and select the layer. Select Image > Adjustments > Curves. In the Curves dialog box, bend the curve into the shape shown here. To do so, click the diagonal line to create points on the curve, and then drag them into position.

Click on OK to apply the changes and invert the colors in the dark areas of the image to brighten the image. The three layers will combine to create a richer image.

The purple hue in the Background copy 2 layer will add dimension to the image.

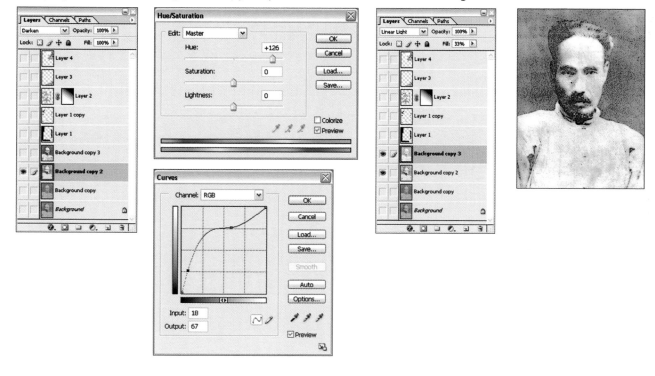

STEP 32. Restoring the Color of the Background Copy 3 Layer

Click on the Background copy 3 layer in the Layers Palette to both redisplay and select the layer. Select Image > Adjustments > Curves. In the Curves dialog box, bend the curve into the shape shown here. To do so, click the diagonal line to create points on the curve, and then drag them into position. Click on OK to apply the changes and invert the colors on the dark areas of the image to brighten it.

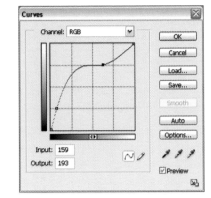

STEP 33. Blending the Black Borders

Click on the Layer 1 layer in the Layers Palette to both redisplay and select the layer. Select Filter > Render > Difference Clouds.

Open the Layer Style drop-down list in the upper-left corner of the Layers Palette, and then click on Multiply. Use the Fill slider on the Layers Palette to change the Fill setting for Layer 1 to 94%.

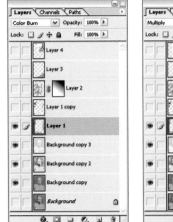

STEP 34. Adjusting the Bouquet Color and Completing the Image

Click on the Layer 3 layer in the Layers Palette to both redisplay and select the layer. Select Image > Adjustments > Hue/Saturation to open the Hue/Saturation dialog box. Drag the Saturation slider to choose the settings shown here, and then click on OK to blend the prominent flowers into the image.

From the File Menu Select Open and open the Book\Sources\Creative Artwork Displacement Map.psd file from the supplementary CD-ROM.

Use the Move Tool to drag the Displace image onto your working image.

The Displace image will appear as layer 5. Move it to the top of the Layers Palette.

Select Edit > Free Transform and scale Layer 5 to cover the whole image.

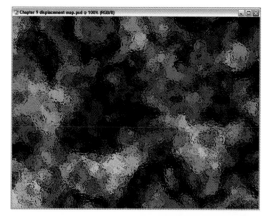

Open the Layer Style drop-down list in the upper-left corner of the Layers Palette, and then select Color Burn. Turn on (show) all the eyeball icons to view every layer.

Effect 14: A Cubic Pipe

In this project, you will use various filters to create a dimensional pipe image. Using Photoshop CS, you can develop an image that is quite different from those made using 3D graphics programs.

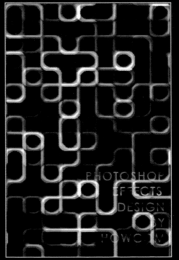

A Cubic Pipe

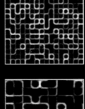
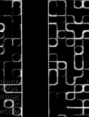

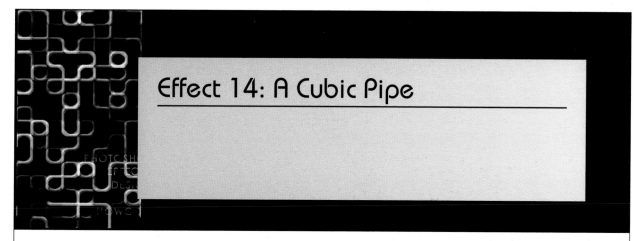

Effect 14: A Cubic Pipe

Total Steps

STEP 1.   Making a New Image

STEP 2.   Adding Noise to the Background Layer

STEP 3.   Blurring the Speckles

STEP 4.   Increasing the Noise Contrast

STEP 5.   Adding a Mosaic Effect

STEP 6.   Outlining the Blocks

STEP 7.   Blurring the Edges

STEP 8.   Emphasizing the Pipes with Directional Lighting

STEP 9.   Brightening the Pipes

STEP 10. Scaling the Pipes

STEP 11. Adding a Black Background Layer

STEP 12. Changing the Color of the Pipes to Blue

STEP 13. Entering Evenly Spaced Text

STEP 14. Moving Individual Letters

STEP 15. Inverting the Copied Image in the Pipe Layer

STEP 16. Making Black Pipes

STEP 17. Blurring the Black Pipes

STEP 18. Blending the Pipe Shadows

STEP 19. Modifying the Text Color to Complete the Image

STEP 1. Making a New Image

Select File > New to open the New dialog box. Set the Width to 400 pixels and the Height to 600 pixels. Set the Resolution to 150 pixels/inch. Make sure that White is selected for Background Contents, and click on OK to create a new image.

STEP 2. Adding Noise to the Background Layer

Select Filter > Noise > Add Noise to open the Add Noise dialog box. Click on the Monochromatic check box if it is not already selected. Set the Amount to 146%, and then click on OK to fill the Background layer with the black and white noise.

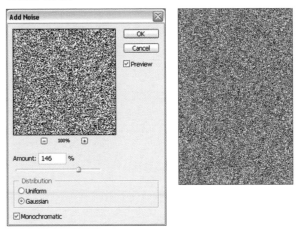

STEP 3. Blurring the Speckles

Select Filter > Blur > Gaussian Blur to open the Gaussian Blur dialog box. Set the Radius to 5.2, and then click on OK to blur the noise speckles together.

STEP 4. Increasing the Noise Contrast

Select Image > Adjustments > Levels to open the Levels dialog box. Drag the Input Levels sliders to the center as shown here, and then click on OK to create a sharp contrast between the black and white areas in the image.

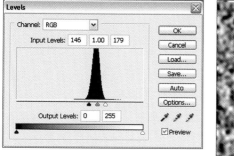 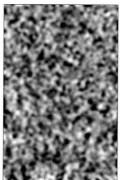

STEP 5. Adding a Mosaic Effect

Select Filter > Pixelate > Mosaic to open the Mosaic dialog box. Set the Cell Size to 25, and then click on OK to cover the Background layer with a mosaic of 25-pixel squares.

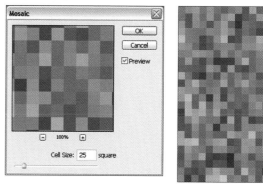

STEP 6. Outlining the Blocks

Select Filter > Stylize > Glowing Edges. Choose the settings shown here in the Glowing Edges dialog box, and then click on OK. Bright edges will appear around the mosaic blocks.

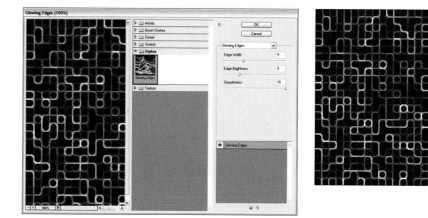

STEP 7. Blurring the Edges

Copy the Background layer by dragging it onto the Create a New Layer button on the Layers Palette.

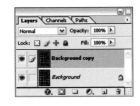

Select Filter > Blur > Gaussian Blur to open the Gaussian Blur dialog box. Set the Radius to 1.5, and then click on OK to blur the image.

STEP 8. Emphasizing the Pipes with Directional Lighting

With the Background copy layer selected in the Layers Palette, select Filter > Render > Lighting Effects to open the Lighting Effects dialog box. Adjust the handles in the Preview area as shown here to redirect the light to shine from the upper-left corner. Choose Red from the Texture Channel drop-down list, and then click on OK to apply the changes to the image, emphasizing the 3D appearance of the pipes.

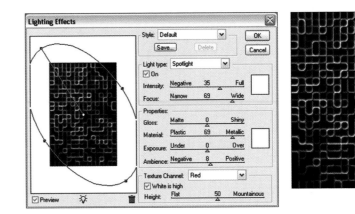

STEP 9. Brightening the Pipes

With the Background copy layer still selected in the Layers Palette, open the Layer Style drop-down list from the upper-left corner of the Layers Palette, and then click on Screen to brighten the pipe image. Click on the Palette Menu button in the upper-right corner of the Layers Palette, and then click on Merge Down to merge both layers onto the Background layer.

STEP 10. Scaling the Pipes

Use the Navigator Palette to zoom the image to 50% size, so that you see some gray work area around the image in the image window.

Choose the Rectangular Marquee Tool from the toolbox, and then drag to select a portion of the image that you want to scale and use in the final composition.

Select Edit > Transform > Scale, press and hold the Shift key, drag to increase the size of the selection in

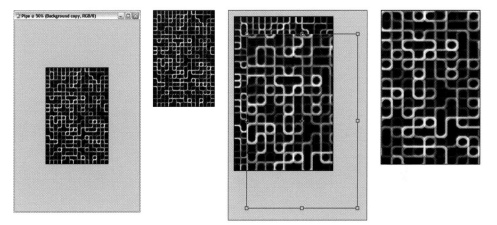

all directions until it fills the image canvas, and then press Enter to finish the transformation. Selecting part of the image and scaling it to a larger size in this way makes the pipe grid appear larger.

STEP 11. Adding a Black Background Layer

Copy the Background layer by dragging it onto the Create a New Layer button on the Layers Palette. Click on the Background layer in the Layers Palette to select that layer. Click on the Default Foreground and Background Colors button in the toolbox, and then use the Paint Bucket Tool or press Alt+Del to fill the Background layer with black. Click on the Background copy layer in the Layers Palette to select that layer.

STEP 12. Changing the Color of the Pipes to Blue

Select Image > Adjustments > Gradient Map from the menu bar to open the Gradient Map dialog box.

Double-click on the gradient in the Gradient Used for Grayscale Mapping box in the Gradient Map dialog box to open the Gradient Editor. Click on the first gradient preset in the Presets area, and then create three more color stops at the bottom of the gradient preview to include additional gradient colors.

To set up a stop, click on the bottom of the gradient preview, and then click on the Color box at the bottom of the panel to open the Color Picker and choose the color for that stop.

Drag the far-right color stop left to move it to the position shown here. (You can delete a color stop by dragging it down off the bottom of the preview.)

Click on OK to close the Gradient Editor, and then click on OK again to apply the gradient.

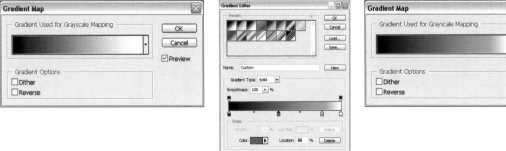
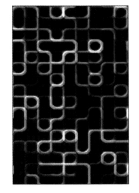

STEP 13. Entering Evenly Spaced Text

Now add text, setting up the letters to fall within the pipes. Choose the Horizontal Type Tool from the toolbox, click on the Toggle the Character and Paragraph Palettes button to open the Character Palette if needed, and then use the Character Palette to choose the settings shown here. Choose a text color that will stand out, such as crimson.

Click on the Right Align Text button on the Options bar. Click to position the insertion point at the right side of the image, and then type the five lines of text shown here, pressing Enter after each line. Click on the Commit Any Current Edits button on the Options bar to finish adding the text. Choose the Move Tool from the toolbox, and then drag the text on the layer so that it fits better within the boxes formed by the pipes, as shown here.

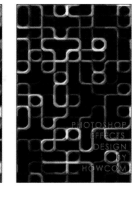

STEP 14. Moving Individual Letters

Even though adjusting the tracking or spacing between characters will help some letters better align vertically with the boxes formed by the pipes, you need to move other letters individually to align them. Right-click on the text layer in the Layers Palette, and then click on Rasterize Layer in the menu that appears. The vector text layer will convert to a regular bitmap layer.

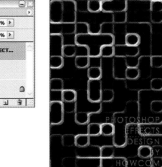
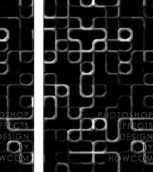

Choose the Rectangular Marquee Tool from the toolbox and drag over a letter to select it.

Choose the Move Tool from the toolbox, and then press the up and down arrow keys to position the letter. (Zoom in on the image to see your work in greater detail.) Repeat the process to position other letters.

Choose Select > Deselect to remove the selection marquee after you position the last letter.

STEP 15. Inverting the Copied Image in the Pipe Layer

You want the letters to appear in the background and be hidden slightly by the pipe shadows. Copy the Background copy layer by dragging it onto the Create a New Layer button on the Layers Palette. With the new Background copy 2 layer still selected in the Layers Palette, choose Image > Adjustments > Invert to invert the layer's colors.

 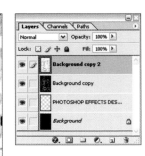

Next, choose Image > Adjustments > Desaturate to convert the layer to a black and white image. Drag the text layer below the Background copy layer in the Layers Palette.

STEP 16. Making Black Pipes

With the Background copy 2 layer still selected in the Layers Palette, choose Image > Adjustments > Levels to open the Levels dialog box. Drag the Input Levels sliders to the positions shown here, and then click on OK to emphasize the black areas in the layer.

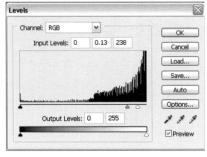 

STEP 17. Blurring the Black Pipes

With the Background copy 2 layer still selected in the Layers Palette, choose Filter > Blur > Gaussian Blur to open the Gaussian Blur dialog box. Set the Radius to 3, and then click on OK to soften the black pipes.

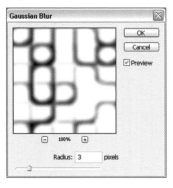 

STEP 18. Blending the Pipe Shadows

Drag the Background copy 2 layer below the Background copy layer in the Layers Palette.

Click on the Background copy layer in the Layers Palette, open the Layer Style drop-down list from the upper-left corner of the Layers Palette, and then click on Screen.

Click on the Background copy 2 layer in the Layers Palette, open the Layer Style drop-down list from the upper-left corner of the Layers Palette, and then click on Multiply. Choose the Move Tool from the toolbox, and drag the Background copy 2 layer slightly down and to the right to emphasize the shadows on the text.

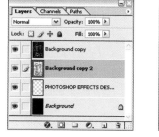

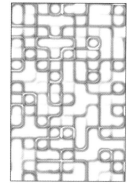
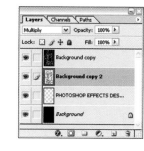

STEP 19. Modifying the Text Color to Complete the Image

Click on the text layer in the Layers Palette to select the layer. Choose Image > Adjustments > Desaturate to convert the letters to gray.

Choose the Rectangular Marquee Tool from the toolbox and drag to select a word or two of text to recolor. Choose Image > Adjustments > Hue/Saturation to open the Hue/Saturation dialog box.

Click on the Colorize check box to select it, drag the sliders to specify the settings shown here, and then click on OK to apply the color to the selection.

Choose Select > Deselect to remove the selection marquee.

Effect 15: Engraving Collage

In this project, you will convert pictures of people to black and white, and then adjust the image levels to create an engraved collage. You will combine the photos in a single image, use variation modes, and then add a bluish tone and text to complete the image.

Effect 15: Engraving Collage

Total Steps

STEP 1.   Opening the Source Photos

STEP 2.   Making the First Image Black and White

STEP 3.   Making the Second Image Black and White

STEP 4.   Removing the Black Background from the Second Image

STEP 5.   Making the Third Image Black and White

STEP 6.   Removing the Black Background from the Third Image

STEP 7.   Making a New Blue Image

STEP 8.   Selecting Vertical Strips

STEP 9.   Filling the Vertical Strips with Gray

STEP 10. Blending the Gray Strips

STEP 11. Adding Black Rectangles

STEP 12. Blending the Black Rectangles

STEP 13. Blending the Third Image

STEP 14. Rotating the New Layer

STEP 15. Blending the First Image

STEP 16. Blending the Second Image

STEP 17. Adding Black Text to Complete the Image

STEP 1. Opening the Source Photos

Select File > Open to open the Book\Sources\Raw Image A (first man).jpg, Book\Sources\Raw Image B (second man).jpg, and Book\Sources\Raw Image C (third man).jpg files from the supplementary CD-ROM.

STEP 2. Making the First Image Black and White

Select Window > Raw Image A (first man).jpg to select the first image file. Select Image > Adjustments > Desaturate to convert the image to black and white.

Select Image > Adjustments > Levels to open the Levels dialog box. Move the Input Levels sliders toward the center as shown here, and then click on OK to eliminate the gray tones from the image.

STEP 3. Making the Second Image Black and White

Select Window > Raw Image B (second man).jpg to select the second image file.

Select Image > Adjustments > Desaturate to convert the image to black and white.

Select Image > Adjustments > Levels to open the Levels dialog box. Move the Input Levels sliders toward the center as shown here, and then click on OK to eliminate the gray tones from the image.

STEP 4. Removing the Black Background from the Second Image

Choose the Brush Tool from the toolbox. Click on the down arrow to open the Brush Preset Picker, double-click on the Spatter 46 Pixels brush type to choose that brush, and then close the Brush Preset Picker.

Set the foreground color to white, and then use the Brush Tool to cover the background with rough white brush strokes. Some black areas will show here and there.

STEP 5. Making the Third Image Black and White

Select Window > Raw Image C (third man).jpg to select the third image file.

Select Image > Adjustments > Desaturate to convert the image to black and white.

Select Image > Adjustments > Levels to open the Levels dialog box. Move the Input Levels sliders toward the center as shown here, and then click on OK to eliminate the gray tones from the image.

STEP 6. Removing the Black Background from the Third Image

Choose the Brush Tool from the toolbox. With the Spatter 46 Pixels brush still selected and the foreground color still set to white, use the Brush Tool to cover the background with rough white brush strokes as before. Some black areas will show here and there.

STEP 7. Making a New Blue Image

Select File > New to open the New dialog box. Set the Width to 800 pixels, the Height to 485 pixels, and the Resolution to 150 pixels/inch. Set Background Contents to White, and then click on OK to open the new image window.

Use the Color Palette to set the foreground color to blue (RGB=0, 121, 255). Use the Paint Bucket Tool or press Alt+Del to fill the new image with blue.

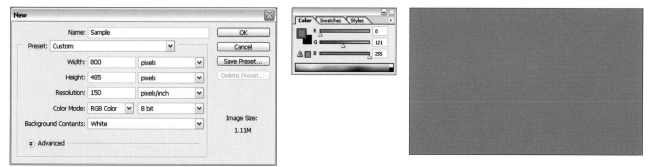

STEP 8. Selecting Vertical Strips

Choose the Rectangular Marquee Tool from the toolbox, and then select the vertical areas shown here. (After you select the first area, press and hold the Shift key as you make the other selections.)

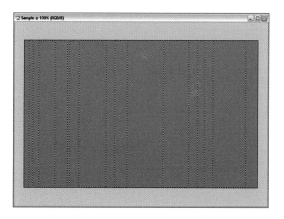

STEP 9. Filling the Vertical Strips with Gray

Click on the Create a New Layer button in the Layers Palette to add a new layer named Layer 1. Use the Color Palette to set the foreground color to a dark gray (RGB=125, 123, 125).

Use the Paint Bucket Tool or press Alt+Del to fill the selection marquee with gray on the new layer. Choose Select > Deselect to remove the selection marquee.

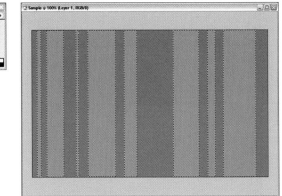

STEP 10. Blending the Gray Strips

With Layer 1 still selected in the Layers Palette, click on the Add a Layer Style button, and then click on Blending Options. Choose Multiply from the Blend Mode drop-down list in the Layer Style dialog box, change the Fill setting to 22%, and then click on OK. The gray strips will blend with the blue background to form lighter and darker strips.

STEP 11. Adding Black Rectangles

Choose the Rectangular Marquee Tool from the toolbox and select the rectangular areas shown here. (After you select the first area, press and hold the Shift key as you make the other selections.) Click on the Background layer in the Layers Palette, and then click on the Create a New Layer button to add a new layer named Layer 2.

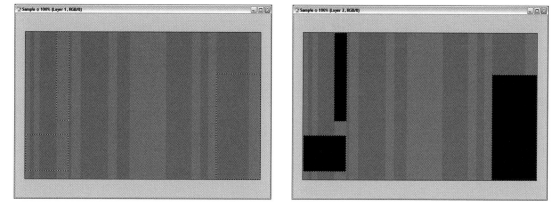

Click on the Default Foreground and Background Colors button in the toolbox to set the foreground color to black. Use the Paint Bucket Tool or press Alt+Del to fill in the selection with black on the new layer.

Choose Select > Deselect to remove the selection marquee.

STEP 12. Blending the Black Rectangles

With Layer 2 still selected in the Layers Palette, click on the Add a Layer Style button, and then click on Blending Options. Choose Color Burn from the Blend Mode drop-down list in the Layer Style dialog box, and then click on OK. The black rectangles will change to a dark blue and blend with the background.

STEP 13. Blending the Third Image

Position the image windows so you can see the windows for both the blue image (where you'll be building the collage now) and Raw Image C (third man).jpg. Choose the Move Tool from the toolbox, and then drag the Background layer of Raw Image C (third man).jpg from the Layers Palette to the window for the blue image. This will copy the picture into a new layer named Layer 3 in the collage image file. Use the Move Tool to position the Layer 3 content in the center of the image.

Select Edit > Free Transform, drag the handles to resize the man's image as shown here, and then press Enter.

With Layer 3 still selected in the Layers Palette, click on the Add a Layer Style button, and then click on Blending Options. Choose Color Burn from the Blend Mode drop-down list in the Layer Style dialog box, and then click on OK. The man's image will change to a dark blue and blend with the background.

STEP 14. Rotating the New Layer

With Layer 3 still selected in the Layers Palette, choose Edit > Transform > Rotate 180° from the menu bar. The man's image will flip on the layer.

STEP 15. Blending the First Image

Position the image windows so you can see the windows for both the collage image and Raw Image A (first man).jpg. Choose the Move Tool from the toolbox, and then drag the Background layer of Raw Image A (first man).jpg from the Layers Palette to the window for the blue image. This will copy the picture into a new layer named Layer 4 in the collage image file.

Use the Move Tool to position the Layer 4 content at the left side of the image.

Select Edit > Free Transform, drag the handles to resize the man's image as shown here, and then press Enter.

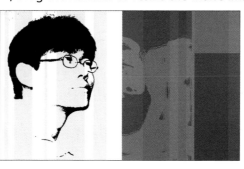
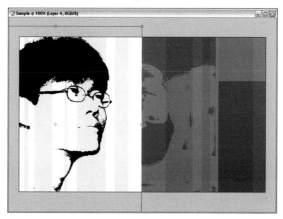

With Layer 4 still selected in the Layers Palette, click on the Add a Layer Style button, and then click on Blending Options. Choose Multiply from the Blend Mode drop-down list in the Layer Style dialog box, and then click on OK. The white areas of the man's image will become transparent.

STEP 16. Blending the Second Image

Position the image windows so you can see the windows for both the collage image and Raw Image B (second man).jpg. Choose the Move Tool from the toolbox, and then drag the Background layer from the Layers Palette of Raw Image B (second man).jpg to the window for the blue image. This will copy the picture into a new layer named Layer 5 in the collage image file.

Use the Move tool to position the Layer 5 content at the right side of the image.

Select Edit > Free Transform, drag the handles to resize the man's image as shown here, and then press Enter.

With Layer 5 still selected in the Layers palette, click on the Add a Layer Style button, and then click on Blending Options. Choose Multiply from the Blend Mode drop-down list in the Layer Style dialog box, and then click on OK.

STEP 17. Adding Black Text to Complete the Image

Use the Horizontal Type Tool and the Character Palette to add text of various sizes to the image, as shown here. Select > Transform > Rotate 180° to flip text on its layer as needed.

Effect 16: Basic Photo Repair

Digital cameras enable you to take quick and easy snapshots without having to fiddle with numerous settings. (You can change the settings on most cameras if you prefer not to use the automatic mode.) Sometimes, due to inadequate lighting or focus, the subject of the photograph will appear too dark or blurred. Using Photoshop CS's powerful photo correction features, you can convert a picture with improper exposure into a professional-quality image.

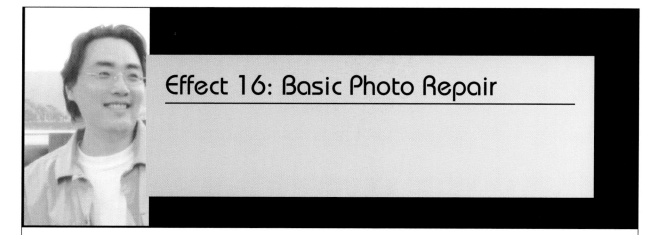

Effect 16: Basic Photo Repair

Total Steps

STEP 1.   Correcting the Source Photo's Brightness

STEP 2.   Sharpening the Image

STEP 3.   Adjusting the Image Color

STEP 4.   Removing Grain and Making Additional Color Corrections

STEP 5.   Removing Fine Lines Using the Healing Brush

STEP 6.   Restoring the Face

STEP 7.   Starting the Liquify Filter to Reshape the Face

STEP 8.   Reshaping the Cheek and Neck

STEP 9.   Comparing Facial Contours

STEP 10. Copying the Background Layer and Applying Cutout Effects

STEP 11. Adjusting the Colors

STEP 12. Blending the Copied Layer

STEP 13. Blending the Copied Layer to Complete the Image.

STEP 1. Correcting the Source Photo's Brightness

Select File > Open to open the Book\Sources\Photo Repair Raw Image (man).jpg file from the supplementary CD-ROM. Because the picture was taken at night without a flash, it's too dark.

Choose Image > Adjustments > Levels to open the Levels dialog box. Move the center Input Levels slider to the position shown here, and then click on OK to brighten the image.

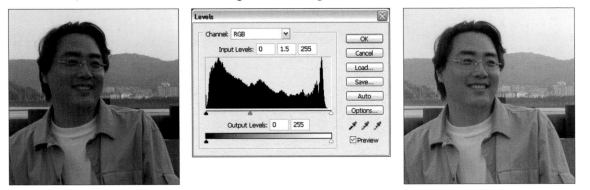

STEP 2. Sharpening the Image

Select Image > Adjustments > Curves to open the Curves dialog box. Bend the curve into the shape shown here. To do so, click on the diagonal line to create points on the curve, and then drag them into position. Click on OK to apply the changes and bring the picture into sharper focus.

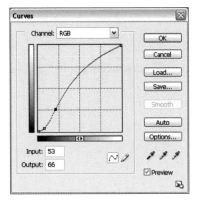

STEP 3. Adjusting the Image Color

Select Image > Adjustments > Auto Color to correct the image automatically using the most optimal colors. However, the image still has strong greenish overtones.

To correct these over-tones, choose Image > Adjustments > Variations to open the Variations dialog box. Click on the More Red and More Yellow thumbnails one time each, and then click on OK to increase the orange tones in the image, restoring its color.

STEP 4. Removing Grain and Making Additional Color Corrections

Some graininess still mars the picture. Choose Filter > Noise > Despeckle, and then press Ctrl+F two times to remove the graininess.

You can now make the image more yellow. Choose Image > Adjustments > Variations to open the Variations dialog box, and then click on OK to enhance the image's yellow tones.

STEP 5. Removing Fine Lines Using the Healing Brush

The Healing Brush Tool enables you to remove imperfections from an image with ease. Use the Navigator Palette to zoom the image to 200% and center the man's face in the image window. Then, choose the Healing Brush Tool from the toolbox.

Hold down the Alt key and click on a rather clean spot in the face to load a repair source for the brush, and then click or drag on the lines and imperfections. (If necessary, use the Brush Preset Picker to choose alternative brush sizes.)

Hold down the Alt key and click on additional locations to load repair sources with different color values. Like the Clone Stamp Tool, the Healing Brush Tool will stamp the repair source over the areas specified; in addition, the Healing Brush Tool blends the repair with the surrounding colors to provide the most optimal change.

STEP 6. Restoring the Face

Continue to use the Healing Brush Tool to remove fine imperfections from the man's face. When you are finished, use the Navigator Palette to zoom the image back out to 50% size.

STEP 7. Starting the Liquify Filter to Reshape the Face

Using the Liquify filter, you can change the contours of the man's face. Choose Filter > Liquify from the menu bar to open the Liquify dialog box.

Click on the Zoom Tool in the toolbox at the left side of the dialog box, and then click twice on the right side of the picture to magnify the area shown.

Click on the Freeze Mask Tool in the toolbox.

Drag in the right side of the image preview to apply a mask, shown here in red. The mask will protect the areas surrounding the face so they will not be affected by the Liquify filter.

STEP 8. Reshaping the Cheek and Neck

Click on the Forward Warp Tool in the toolbox at the left, and then use the Tool Options settings at the right side of the dialog box to adjust the brush size, as shown here. Move the mouse pointer just to the right of the man's face, and then drag left to increase the cheek contour, making the man's face appear thinner. Click on the Zoom Tool again, and then hold down the Alt key and click on the image to zoom back out to 100%.

Use the Freeze Mask Tool to mask off the area to the left of the stray hairs on the left side of the man's head, and then use the Warp Tool to push the hairs up to the right.

If desired, you can also mask the man's neck and nape area at the left, and use the Warp Tool to push those areas to the right so the man's neck appears thinner. Click on OK to apply the Liquify changes.

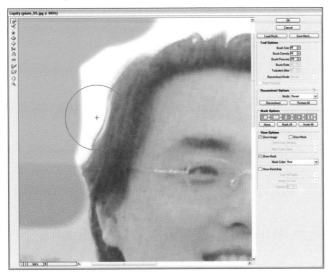

STEP 9. Comparing Facial Contours

Compare the images before and after you applied the Liquify filter. The facial contours look much more attractive in the edited image on the right.

STEP 10. Copying the Background Layer and Applying Cutout Effects

Copy the Background layer by dragging it onto the Create a New Layer button on the Layers Palette. With the new Background copy layer selected in the Layers Palette, choose Filter > Artistic > Cutout from the menu to open the Cutout dialog box. Choose the settings shown here, and then click on OK to simplify the image colors and shapes.

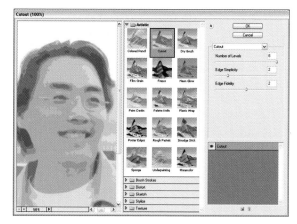

STEP 11. Adjusting the Colors

With the Background copy layer still selected in the Layers Palette, choose Image > Adjustments > Hue/Saturation to open the Hue/Saturation dialog box. Drag the sliders to specify the settings shown here, and then click on OK to give the cutout colors a brownish tint.

STEP 12. Blending the Copied Layer

With the Background copy layer still selected in the Layers Palette, choose Filter > Blur > Gaussian Blur to open the Gaussian Blur dialog box. Set the Radius to 4.4, and then click on OK to blur the cutout image.

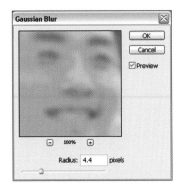

STEP 13. Blending the Copied
Layer to Complete the Image

With the Background copy layer
still selected in the Layers Palette,
click on the Add a Layer Style button, and then click on Blending
Options. Choose Overlay from the
Blend Mode drop-down list in the
Layer Style dialog box, and then
click on OK. Use the Opacity slider
in the Layer Style dialog box to set
the opacity to 57%, further blending the layers for a fantastic result.

Effect 17: 3D Metallic Spheres

In this project, you will see how to use Photoshop CS to create strong 3D objects that previously had to be made using a dedicated 3D graphics program. The red sphere within the collection of 3D metallic spheres brightens the entire image.

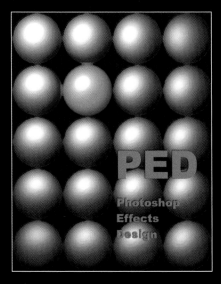

3D Metallic Spheres

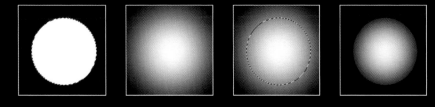

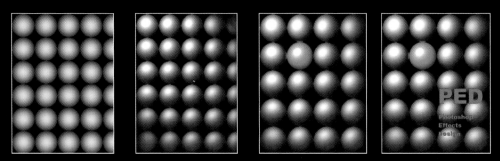

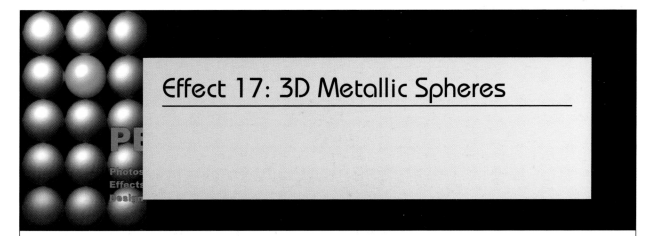

Effect 17: 3D Metallic Spheres

Total Steps

STEP 1.   Making a New Image with a Black Background

STEP 2.   Making a White Circle

STEP 3.   Saving the Selection as an Alpha Channel

STEP 4.   Using the Alpha Channel to Create a Sphere

STEP 5.   Darkening the Sphere

STEP 6.   Refining the Sphere Image

STEP 7.   Saving the Sphere as a Pattern

STEP 8.   Filling the New Image with the Sphere Pattern

STEP 9.   Selecting the Black Areas between the Spheres

STEP 10.   Copying the Layer and Deleting the Black Areas

STEP 11.   Emphasizing the Spheres with Directional Lighting

STEP 12.   Making the Spheres Look Metallic

STEP 13.   Brightening the Metallic Spheres

STEP 14.   Applying Shadows to the Metallic Spheres

STEP 15.   Copying One Metallic Sphere

STEP 16.   Making the Copied Sphere Red

STEP 17.   Adding a Glow to the Red Sphere

STEP 18.   Cropping the Image

STEP 19.   Completing the Image

STEP 1. Making a New Image with a Black Background

Select File > New to open the New dialog box. Set the Width and Height to 200 pixels. Set the Resolution to 150 pixels/inch, make sure that White is selected for Background Contents, and click on OK to create a new image.

Click on the Default Foreground and Background Colors button in the toolbox to set the foreground color to black and the background color to white. Use the Paint Bucket Tool or press Alt+Del to fill the Background layer with black.

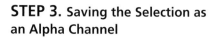

STEP 2. Making a White Circle

Choose the Elliptical Marquee Tool from the toolbox. Press and hold the Shift key, and then drag on the image to draw a perfect circle.

Click on the Switch Foreground and Background Colors button in the toolbox to set the foreground color to white, and then use the Paint Bucket Tool or press Alt+Del to fill the selection with white.

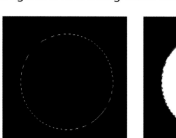

STEP 3. Saving the Selection as an Alpha Channel

Choose Window > Channels to open the Channels Palette, and then click on the Save Selection as Channel button on the palette. An alpha channel named Alpha 1 will appear in the palette.

Choose Select > Deselect to remove the selection marquee.

Choose Filter > Blur > Gaussian Blur to open the Gaussian Blur dialog box. Set the Radius to 30, and then click on OK to blur the circle image.

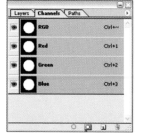

STEP 4. Using the Alpha Channel to Create a Sphere

Hold down the Ctrl key and click on the Alpha 1 channel in the Channels Palette to load the alpha channel as a selection. Choose Select > Inverse to invert the selection.

With the foreground color still set to white, press the Del key to delete the area in the selection, making it black. Choose Select > Deselect to remove the selection marquee.

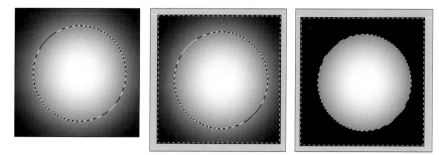

STEP 5. Darkening the Sphere

Select Window > Layers to redisplay the Layers Palette.

Select Image > Adjustments > Curves. In the Curves dialog box, bend the curve into the shape shown here. To do so, click on the diagonal line to create a point on the curve, and then drag it into position. Click on OK to apply the changes and emphasize the dark areas of the sphere.

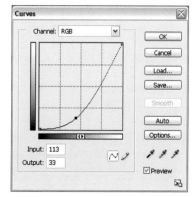

STEP 6. Refining the Sphere Image

Select Window > Channels to return to the Channels Palette. Hold down the Ctrl key and click on the Alpha 1 channel to load the channel as a selection. Select Image > Crop to crop the image to a tight size surrounding the selection.

Choose Select > Deselect to remove the selection marquee. Select Window > Layers to redisplay the Layers Palette.

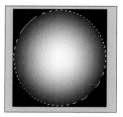

STEP 7. Saving the Sphere as a Pattern

Select Edit > Define Pattern to open the Pattern Name dialog box. Type **Ball** as the pattern name, and then click on OK to save the pattern. Select File > New to open the New dialog box. Set the Width to 600 pixels and the Height to 800 pixels. Set the Resolution to 150 pixels/inch, make sure that White is selected for Background Contents, and click on OK to create a new image.

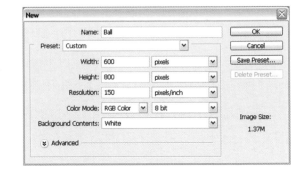

STEP 8. Filling the New Image with the Sphere Pattern

Select Edit > Fill to open the Fill dialog box. Choose Pattern from the Use drop-down list, click on the Custom Pattern box to open a palette of patterns, and then double-click on the Ball pattern you saved in Step 7. Click on OK to fill the Background layer of the new image with the sphere pattern.

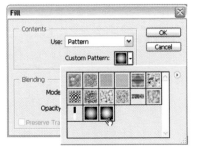

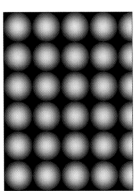

STEP 9. Selecting the Black Areas between the Spheres

Choose Select > Color Range to open the Color Range dialog box. Click on a black area between spheres in the image window, change the Fuzziness setting in the dialog box to 45, and then click on OK to select only the black background areas.

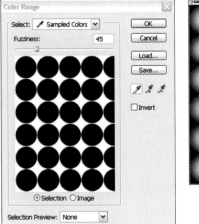

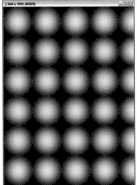

STEP 10. Copying the Layer and Deleting the Black Areas

Copy the Background layer by dragging it onto the Create a New Layer button on the Layers Palette. With the new Background copy layer still selected in the Layers Palette, press the Del key to delete the selected black areas. Click on the eye icon beside the Background layer in the Layers Palette to hide that layer from view.

After verifying the result, redisplay the Background layer by clicking the eye icon box beside the layer in the Layers Palette. Choose Select > Deselect to remove the selection marquee.

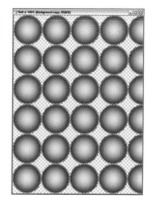

STEP 11. Emphasizing the Spheres with Directional Lighting

Click on the Background copy layer in the Layers Palette to select that layer. Select Filter > Render > Lighting Effects to open the Lighting Effects dialog box. Adjust the handles in the Preview area as shown here to redirect the light to shine from the upper-left corner. Choose Red from the Texture Channel drop-down list, and then click on OK to apply the changes to the image, emphasizing the 3D appearance of the spheres.

STEP 12. Making the Spheres Look Metallic

With the Background copy layer still selected in the Layers Palette, select Filter > Artistic > Palette Knife to open the Palette Knife dialog box. Choose the settings shown here, and then click on OK.

Leaving the Background copy layer selected, select Filter > Noise > Median to open the Median dialog box. Set the Radius to 4, and then click on OK.

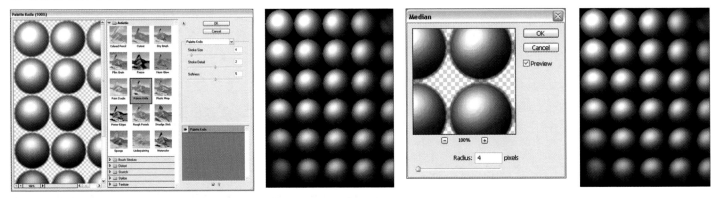

STEP 13. Brightening the Metallic Spheres

The metal spheres look too heavy. With the Background copy layer still selected in the Layers Palette, select Image > Adjustments > Levels to open the Levels dialog box. Drag the left Output Levels slider to the position shown here, and then click on OK to brighten the image so the edges of the spheres become more apparent.

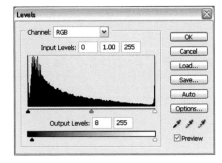

STEP 14. Applying Shadows to the Metallic Spheres

With the Background copy layer selected in the Layers Palette, click on the Add a Layer Style button on the Palette, and then click on Inner Shadow to open the Layer Style dialog box. Choose the settings shown here, and then click on OK to emphasize the shadows in the lower-right areas of the spheres, opposite the light source.

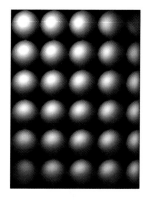

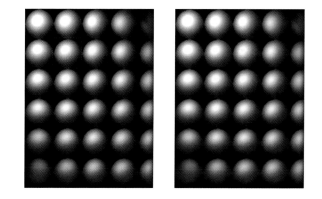

STEP 15. Copying One Metallic Sphere

Choose the Rectangular Marquee Tool from the toolbox and drag to select one of the spheres near the top of the image. Press Ctrl+C to copy the selection, and then press Ctrl+V to paste the selected metal sphere onto a new layer named Layer 1.

STEP 16. Making the Copied Sphere Red

Click to select the new Layer 1 layer in the Layers Palette, if necessary. Select Image > Adjustments > Variations to open the Variations dialog box. Click on the More Red and More Yellow thumbnails as many times as needed until the sphere in the Current Pick thumbnail turns red. Click on OK.

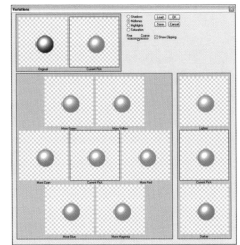

In the Layers Palette, drag the Inner Shadow effect from the Background copy layer to the Layer 1 layer to copy the inner shadow effect to the red sphere.

STEP 17. Adding a Glow to the Red Sphere

With the Layer 1 layer selected in the Layers Palette, click on the Add a Layer Style button on the palette, and then click on Outer Glow. Choose the settings shown here in the Layer Style dialog box, and then click on OK.

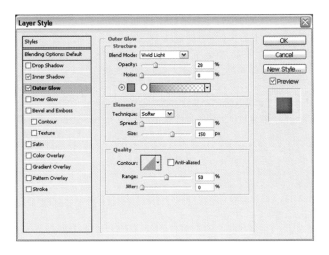

STEP 18. Cropping the Image

Choose the Rectangular Marquee Tool from the toolbox, and then drag to select the desired portion, eliminating any partial spheres. Select Image > Crop to remove areas outside the selection from the image. Choose Select > Deselect to remove the selection marquee.

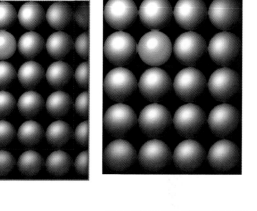

STEP 19. Completing the Image

Use the Horizontal Type Tool and the Character Palette to add simple red text to the completed image. Also, add a drop shadow to the text layer to emphasize the 3D appearance of the image.

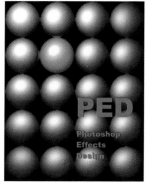

Movement

The word tempo is used as
an image as much as a word
throught the combination of
scale with speed
and time.

Effect 18: A Cube Mosaic

In this project, you will fill a layer with cubes and vary their texture and color to create a 3D mosaic effect. Various blending modes emphasize the mosaic texture.

A Cube Mosaic

The word tempo is used as an image as much as a word throught the combination of scale with speed and time.

Movement

Movement

Effect 18: A Cube Mosaic

Mov

Total Steps

STEP 1. Making a New Image with a Black Background

STEP 2. Adding Black and White Noise

STEP 3. Creating Mosaic Tiles

STEP 4. Adding Dimension to the Tiles

STEP 5. Adding and Blending a Cloud Texture Layer

STEP 6. Adding Color to the Tiles

STEP 7. Adding a Turquoise Layer

STEP 8. Blending the Turquoise Layer

STEP 9. Adding a Semitransparent White Band

STEP 10. Adding and Resizing the Title

STEP 11. Making the First Letter Brown

STEP 12. Adding the Remaining Text

STEP 13. Adding a Human Shape to Complete the Image

STEP 1. Making a New Image with a Black Background

Select File > New from the menu bar to open the New dialog box. Set the Width to 800 pixels and the Height to 600 pixels. Set the Resolution to 100 pixels/inch, make sure that White is selected for Background Contents, and click on OK to create a new image.

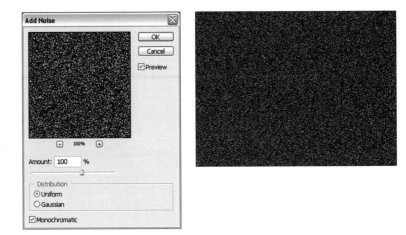

Click on the Default Foreground and Background Colors button in the toolbox to set the foreground color to black, and then use the Paint Bucket Tool or press Alt+Del to fill the Background layer with black.

STEP 2. Adding Black and White Noise

Select Filter > Noise > Add Noise from the menu bar to open the Noise dialog box. Click on the Monochromatic check box to select it, set the Amount to 100, and then click on OK to apply black and white noise to the Background layer.

STEP 3. Creating
Mosaic Tiles

Select Filter > Texture >
Patchwork to open the
Patchwork dialog box.
Choose the settings shown
here, and then click on OK
to fill the Background layer
with uniform mosaic tiles.

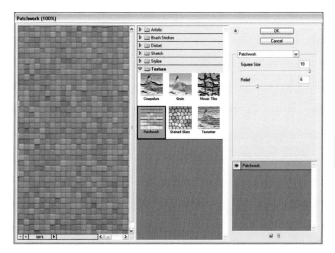

STEP 4. Adding
Dimension to the Tiles

Select Filter > Stylize >
Glowing Edges to open the
Glowing Edges dialog box.
Choose the settings shown
here, and then click on OK
to emphasize some tiles and
add dimension to the
image.

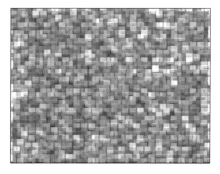

STEP 5. Adding and Blending a Cloud Texture Layer

Click on the Create a New Layer button on the Layers Palette to make a new layer named Layer 1. With the foreground color still set to black, use the Paint Bucket Tool or press Alt+Del to fill Layer 1 with black. Select Filter > Render > Difference Clouds from the menu bar to fill Layer 1 with a cloud pattern.

If desired, reapply (Ctrl+F) and/or remove (Ctrl+Z) until the cloud texture achieves the appearance you prefer.

With Layer 1 still selected in the Layers Palette, open the Layer Style drop-down list from the upper-left corner of the Layers Palette, and then click on Overlay to apply the mottled tones of the clouds to the mosaic.

 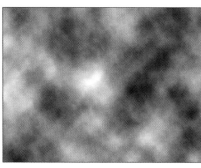  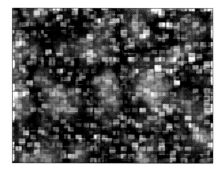

STEP 6. Adding Color to the Tiles

Click on the Create New Fill or Adjustment Layer button on the Layers Palette, and then click on Gradient Map in the menu that appears. The Gradient Map dialog box will open.

Click on the gradient in the Gradient Used for Grayscale Mapping box of the Gradient Map dialog box to open the Gradient Editor dialog box. Click on the first gradient preset in the Presets area, and then create three more color stops at the bottom of the gradient preview to include additional gradient colors. To set up a stop, click on the bottom of the gradient preview, and then click on the Color box at the bottom of the dialog box to open the Color Picker and choose the color for that stop. Drag the far-right color stop left to move it to the position shown here. (You can delete a color stop by dragging it down off the bottom of the preview.)

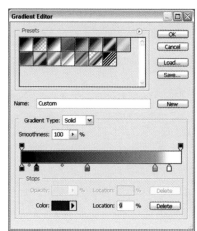

Click on OK to close the Gradient Editor dialog box, and then click on OK again to apply the gradient.

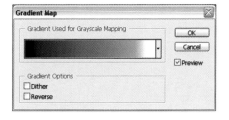

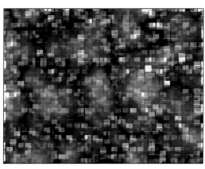

STEP 7. Adding a Turquoise Layer

Click on the Create a New Layer button on the Layers Palette to add a new layer named Layer 2. Use the Color Palette to set the foreground color to turquoise (RGB=3, 158, 160).

Use the Paint Bucket Tool or press Alt +Del to fill the layer with turquoise.

Move Layer 2 so it is directly above Layer 1 and below the Gradient Map.

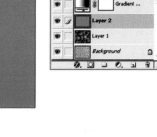

STEP 8. Blending the Turquoise Layer

With Layer 2 still selected in the Layers Palette, open the Layer Style drop-down list from the upper-left corner of the Layers Palette, and then click on Overlay to mix the turquoise color with the mosaic.

STEP 9. Adding a Semitransparent White Band

Click on the Create a New Layer button on the Layers Palette to add a new layer named Layer 3, and make sure it is above the Gradient Map layer.

Set the foreground color to white. Choose the Rectangular Marquee Tool from the toolbox, drag to select a wide band across the image, and then use the Paint Bucket Tool or press Alt+Del to fill the selection with white.

Choose Select > Deselect from the menu bar to remove the selection marquee. With Layer 3 still selected, use the Opacity slider on the Layers Palette to change the Layer 3 Opacity setting to 70%.

   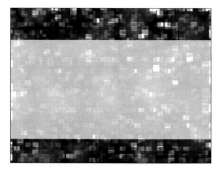

STEP 10. Adding and Resizing the Title

Click on the Default Foreground and Background Colors button in the toolbox to set the foreground color to black. Choose the Horizontal Type Tool from the toolbox, click on the Toggle the Character and Paragraph Palettes button to open the Character Palette (if needed), and then use the Character Palette to choose a font and font size. Click on the image, type **Movement** as the title, and then click on the Commit Any Current Edits button on the Options bar to finish adding the title.

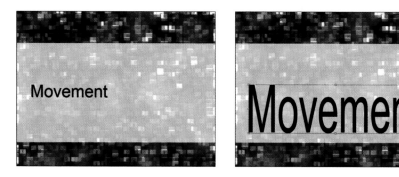

Select Edit > Transform > Scale from the menu bar, drag the handles to increase the text size to fill the white band, and then press Enter to finish the transformation.

STEP 11. Making the First Letter Brown

With the Horizontal Type Tool still selected, drag over the letter M on the Movement layer.

Use the Color Palette to specify a dark brown color (RGB=159, 16, 0), and then click on the Commit Any Current Edits button on the Options bar to finish applying the brown color to the letter M.

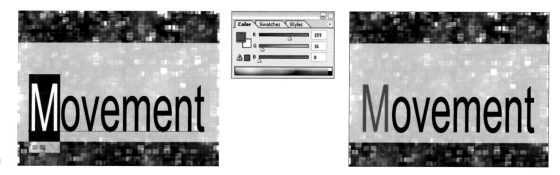

STEP 12. Adding the Remaining Text

Create a new text layer by selecting the Horizontal Type Tool and entering the copy shown. Choose the font settings shown here in the Character Palette.

Click on the Paragraph Palette tab, and then click on the Right Align Text button. Then, click on the new layer, type the remaining text as shown here, and click on the Commit Any Current Edits button on the Options bar.

STEP 13. Adding a Human Shape to Complete the Image

Use the Color Palette to set the foreground color to a blue-green color (RGB=0, 116, 159).

Choose the Pen Tool from the toolbox, and then click on the Add New Layer button in the Layers Palette and make sure it is above the other layers. Draw a simple human shape at the right side of the image, as shown here. (It might be easier if you make the new layer the only visible layer, as shown here.)

With the Shape 1 layer still selected in the Layers Palette, open the Layer Style drop-down list from the upper-left corner of the Layers Palette, and then click on Linear Light. Also, use the Fill slider on the Layers Palette to change the Fill setting for the layer to 75%, blending the person nicely with the rest of the image. (To hide the path points, choose Window > Paths, click on a gray area within the palette, and then choose Window > Layers to redisplay the Layers Palette.)

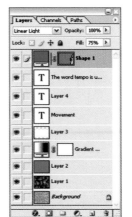

News: Contact:

Effect 19: Wire Frame Bridge

You can use Photoshop's Brush Tool to create a wire frame effect that normally requires a 3D graphics program. In this project, you will create a wire frame bridge.

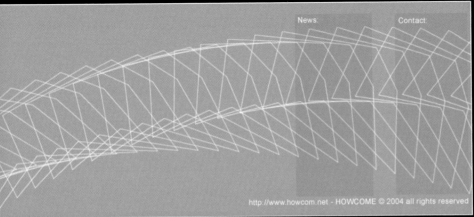

Wire Frame Bridge

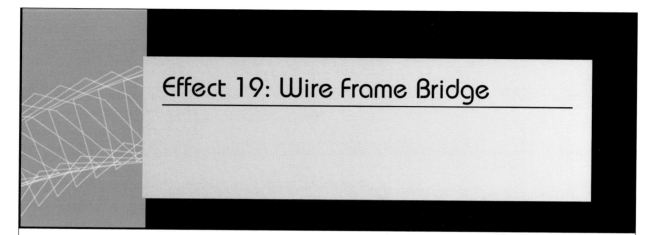

Effect 19: Wire Frame Bridge

Total Steps

STEP 1.   Making a New Image with a Pea-Green Background

STEP 2.   Creating the Wire Frame Shape on a New Layer

STEP 3.   Saving the Wire Frame as a Brush

STEP 4.   Selecting the Wire Frame Brush

STEP 5.   Adding Rotation to the Brush

STEP 6.   Stroking the Path with the Wire Frame Brush

STEP 7.   Selecting Two Rectangles

STEP 8.   Filling the Rectangles

STEP 9.   Adding Text to Complete the Image

STEP 1. Making a New Image with a Pea-Green Background

Select File > New to open the New dialog box. Set the Width to 800 pixels and the Height to 350 pixels. Set the Resolution to 150 pixels/inch, make sure that White is selected under Background Contents, and then click on OK to create a new image.

Use the Color Palette to set the foreground color to a dark pea-green (RGB=136, 136, 0), and then use the Paint Bucket Tool or press Alt+Del to fill the Background layer with the green color.

STEP 2. Creating the Wire Frame Shape on a New Layer

Click on the Create a New Layer button in the Layers Palette to add a new layer named Layer 1. Choose the Paint Brush Tool from the toolbox.

Click on the down arrow for the Brush Preset Picker on the Options bar, drag the Master Diameter slider to set the brush size to 1, and then close the Brush Preset Picker.

Click on the Default Foreground and Background Colors button on the toolbox to reset the foreground color to black, and then use the Navigator Palette to zoom in.

Draw the shape shown here by clicking for the first point, and then pressing and holding the Shift key and clicking to make additional points. Note that the 1-pixel pointer will be difficult to see on the green background.

STEP 3. Saving the Wire Frame as a Brush

With the Layer 1 layer still selected in the Layers Palette, choose Select > Load Selection.

Make sure Layer 1 Transparency is selected from the Channel drop-down list, and then click on OK to select the wire frame shape on the layer. Select Edit > Define Brush Preset from the menu bar to open the Brush Name dialog box.

Type a new name for the brush, if desired, and then click on OK to save the shape as a brush. Choose Select > Deselect to remove the selection marquee.

STEP 4. Selecting the Wire Frame Brush

Choose the Brush Tool from the toolbox and click on the Toggle the Brushes Palette button on the Options bar.

Click on Brush Presets at the top of the list at the left, scroll down the list of brushes at the right, and click on the new brush at the bottom of the list. Click on Brush Tip Shape in the list at the left, and then set the Spacing to 9%.

STEP 5. Adding Rotation to the Brush

Click on Shape Dynamics in the list at the left side of the Brushes Palette. Open the Control drop-down list under Angle Jitter, and then click on Fade in the drop-down list. This will select the value in the text box to the right of the Control drop-down list. Type **100** to replace the existing value. This setting will cause the brush angle to rotate slowly, making one revolution per 100 repetitions of the shape when you drag the brush.

Click outside the Brushes Palette to close the palette.

Click the Layer Visibility icon beside Layer 1 in the Layers Palette to hide that layer. Click on the Create a New Layer button on the Layers Palette to add a new layer named Layer 2.

Choose the Pen Tool from the toolbox, and then click on the Paths button on the Options bar to specify that you want to draw a work path. Use the Pen Tool to draw the path shown here. (Zoom out if necessary.) Then, use the Direct Selection Tool from the toolbox to drag the handles on either end of the path to adjust the shape of the path. Press Enter to finish editing the path.

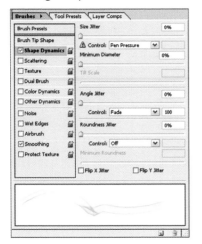

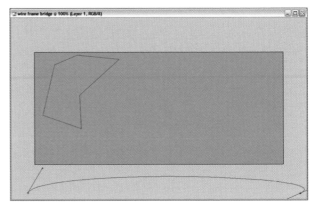

STEP 6. Stroking the Path with the Wire Frame Brush

Select Window > Paths from the menu bar to open the Paths Palette. The path you just drew will appear as a path named Work Path.

Set the foreground color to white, and then choose the Brush Tool from the toolbox. The Brush box on the Options bar will show that the wire frame brush you made earlier is still selected as the current brush.

Click on the Work Path choice in the Paths layer, and then click on the Stroke Path with Brush button at the bottom of the palette. A wire frame bridge will appear along the path.

Click in the gray area below the path in the Paths Palette to hide the path. Select Window > Layers to redisplay the Layers Palette.

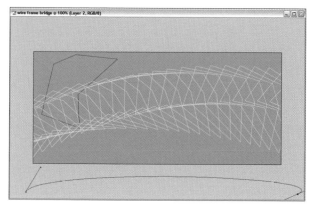

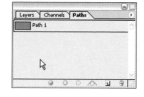

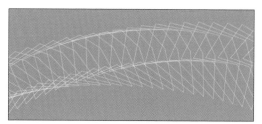

STEP 7. Selecting Two Rectangles

Click on the Create a New Layer button on the Layers Palette to add a new layer named Layer 3.

Choose the Rectangular Marquee Tool from the toolbox and drag to select two rectangles at the right side of the image, as shown here. Press and hold the Shift key after you draw the first rectangle to add the second rectangle.

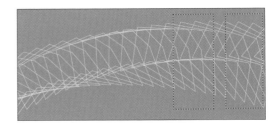

STEP 8. Filling the Rectangles

Use the Color Palette to set the foreground color to a yellow-green, and then use the Paint Bucket Tool or press Alt+Del to fill the selection with yellow-green.

With Layer 3 still selected in the Layers Palette, open the Layer Style drop-down list in the upper-left corner of the Layers Palette, and then click on Soft Light to blend the blocks of color.

Choose Select > Deselect from the menu bar to remove the selection marquee.

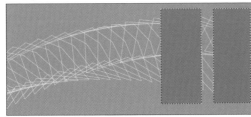

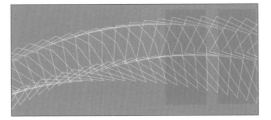

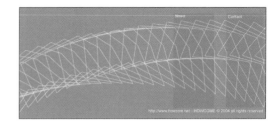

STEP 9. Adding Text to Complete the Image

Use the Horizontal Type Tool and the Character Palette to add text in a bright yellow-green color to complete the image, as shown here. You could use an image like this as a sub-page for a Web site.

Take it easy...
Smile
Face

Effect 20: Smile Face

Take a picture snapped on the streets using a digital camera and turn it into an elegant Web image. Using various filters, such as Cutout and Dry Brush, and various layer-blending modes, you can create a simple yet effective result. A lined pattern applied to the entire picture makes the image more elegant.

Smile Face

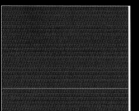

Effect 20: Smile Face

Total Steps

STEP 1.   Blurring the Source Photo

STEP 2.   Applying Cutout Effects to the Image

STEP 3.   Applying Brush Effects to the Image

STEP 4.   Blending the Layers

STEP 5.   Creating the Line Pattern

STEP 6.   Filling Layer 1 with the Pattern

STEP 7.   Blending the Pattern Layer

STEP 8.   Adding a Gradient and Blending the Pattern

STEP 9.   Cropping the Image

STEP 10. Adding Text to Complete the Image

STEP 1. Blurring the Source Photo

Select File > Open to open the Book/Sources/Smile Raw Image (woman).tif file from the supplementary CD-ROM.

Select Filter > Blur > Gaussian Blur to open

the Gaussian Blur dialog box. Set the Radius to approximately 1.4, and then click on OK to blur the image slightly and remove fine particles from the picture.

STEP 2. Applying Cutout Effects to the Image

Copy the Background layer by dragging it onto the Create a New Layer button on the Layers Palette. Click on the eye icon beside the copied layer to hide the layer from view. Then, click on the original Background layer to select it.

Select Filter > Artistic > Cutout to open the Cutout dialog box. Choose the settings shown here, and then click on OK. This will simplify the image so it uses fewer colors, as if it were created from colored paper.

STEP 3.
Applying Brush Effects to the Image

Click on the Background copy layer in the Layers Palette to both redisplay and select the layer.

Select Filter > Artistic > Dry Brush to open the Dry Brush dialog box. Choose the settings shown here, and then click on OK to make the image appear as if it has been painted with a brush.

STEP 4. Blending the Layers

Double-click on the Background copy layer to open the Layer Style dialog box. Choose Overlay from the Blend Mode drop-down list in the Layer Style dialog box, and then click on OK to blend the filter effects applied to the two layers.

STEP 5. Creating the Line Pattern

Click on the Create a New Layer button on the Layers Palette to add a new
layer named Layer 1. Use the
Navigator to zoom the image to its
maximum size (1600%). Click on the
Default Foreground and Background
Colors button in the toolbox to set the
foreground color to black.

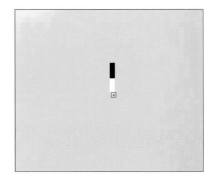

Choose the Pencil Tool from the toolbox, and then click on
the down arrow to open the Brush Preset Picker. Double-click
on the Hard Round one-pixel brush size to select that brush, and then close the palette.

Drag down to color three pixels black, click on the Switch Foreground and Background Colors button in the toolbox to set
the foreground color to white, and then drag to color the next three pixels white. This will create a black and white vertical line, as shown here.

Hold down the Ctrl key and click on
Layer 1 in the Layers Palette to make a
selection in the shape of the vertical
line.

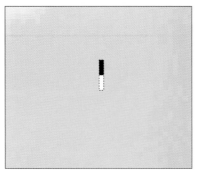

Select Edit > Define Pattern to open the
Pattern Name dialog box. Type Stroke
as the pattern name, and then click on
OK to save the selection as a pattern.

Choose Select > Deselect to remove the
selection marquee.

STEP 6. Filling Layer 1 with the Pattern

Select Edit > Fill to open the Fill dialog box. Choose Pattern from the drop-down list, and then click on the Custom Pattern box.

Double-click on the new Stroke pattern to select it, close the palette, and then click on OK to fill Layer 1 with the pattern. Use the Navigator Palette to zoom back out to 66.67%. The layer will be filled with three-pixel black and white lines.

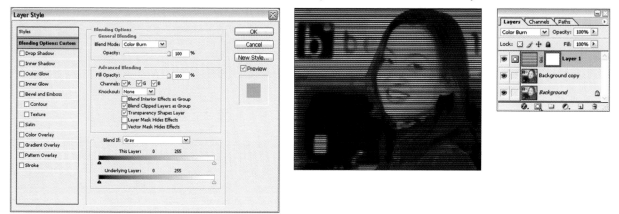

STEP 7. Blending the Pattern Layer

With Layer 1 still selected in the Layers Palette, click on the Add a Layer Style button, and then click on Blending Options. Choose Color Burn from the Blend Mode drop-down list in the Layer Style dialog box. Click on OK to blend the image of the woman and the striped pattern together naturally.

However, the stripes are too dark. Click on the Add Layer Mask button on the Layers Palette to add a mask to the layer.

STEP 8. Adding a Gradient and Blending the Pattern

Notice the icon identical to the Add Layer Mask button that appears beside Layer 1 in the Layers Palette. This indicates that you can edit the layer mask. Set the foreground color to white and the background color to black. Choose the Gradient Tool from the toolbox, and then click on the Linear Gradient button on the Options bar, if necessary.

Drag from an area above and to the left of the woman's head down to just below her chin. Applying the gradient to the mask partially hides the pattern. The white areas of the mask image allow the pattern to appear at full intensity, while the darker regions of the mask prevent the pattern from appearing. Use the Fill slider on the Layers Palette to change the fill setting for Layer 1 to 70%, further blending the pattern.

STEP 9. Cropping the Image

Choose the Rectangular Marquee Tool from the toolbox. Select the portion of the image shown here. Select Image > Crop to remove the content outside the selection from the image file. Choose Select > Deselect to remove the selection marquee.

STEP 10. Adding Text to Complete the Image

Complete the image by using the Horizontal Type Tool to add the text shown here. Choose a simple font with white as the text color, and add each line on a separate layer. Use a different font size and line spacing settings for each line. If necessary, use the Edit > Free Transform command to resize and reposition the text so it overlaps slightly.

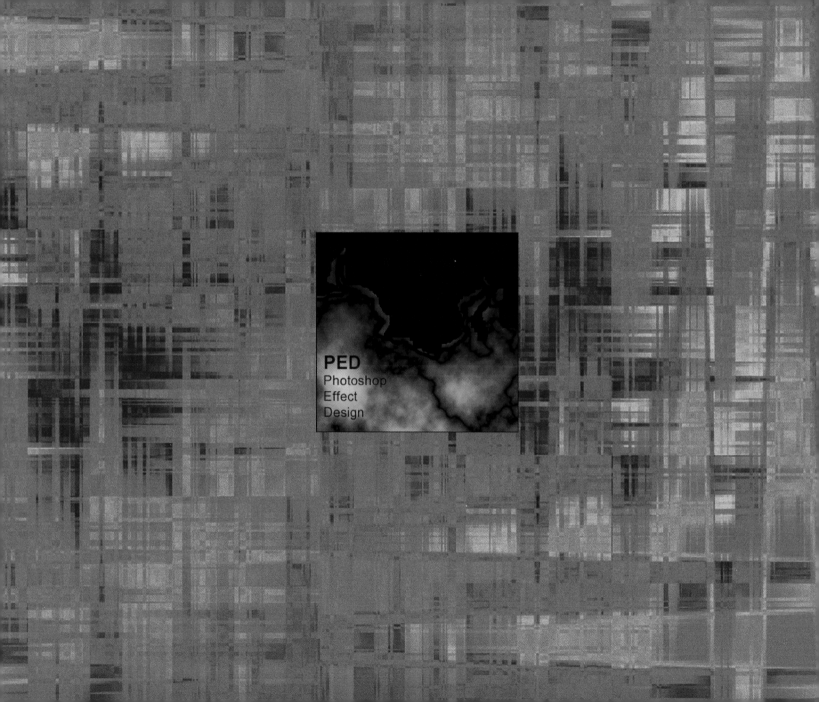

PED

Photoshop
Effect
Design

Effect 21: Realistic Flame

In this project, you will create a burning flame.
You will see how to use the Clouds and Difference
Clouds filters to create this texture.

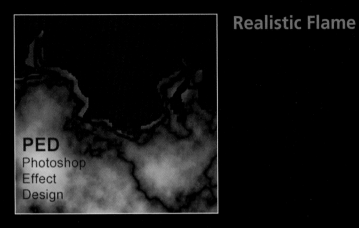

Realistic Flame

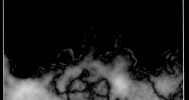 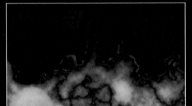 

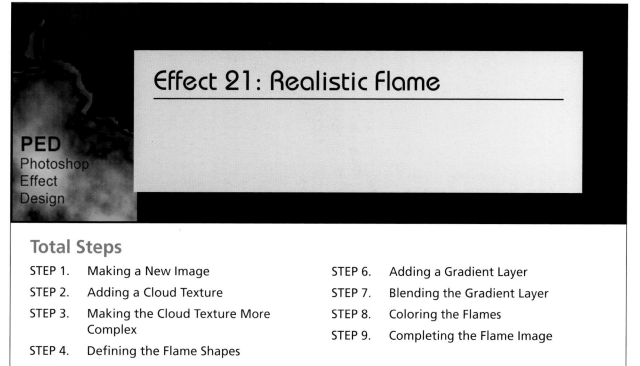

Effect 21: Realistic Flame

PED
Photoshop
Effect
Design

Total Steps

STEP 1. Making a New Image

STEP 2. Adding a Cloud Texture

STEP 3. Making the Cloud Texture More Complex

STEP 4. Defining the Flame Shapes

STEP 5. Removing Unwanted Areas

STEP 6. Adding a Gradient Layer

STEP 7. Blending the Gradient Layer

STEP 8. Coloring the Flames

STEP 9. Completing the Flame Image

STEP 1. Making a New Image

Select File > New to open the New dialog box. Set the Width to 800 pixels and the Height to 450 pixels. Set the Resolution to 150 pixels/inch, make sure that White is selected for Background Contents, and then click on OK to create a new image.

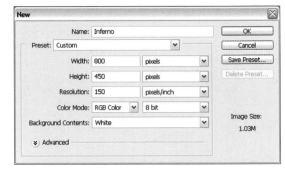

STEP 2. Adding a Cloud Texture

Click on the Default Foreground and Background Colors button in the toolbox to make the foreground color black and the background color white. Select Filter > Render > Clouds from the menu bar to fill the Background layer with a cloud texture. Press Ctrl+F to reapply the filter until the clouds reach the desired appearance.

STEP 3. Making the Cloud Texture More Complex

Select Filter > Render > Difference Clouds from the menu bar. The Difference Clouds filter effect will blend with the Clouds filter effect, creating a more complex shape. Continue to press Ctrl+F (at least three to five times) until you see flame shapes along the bottom of the image.

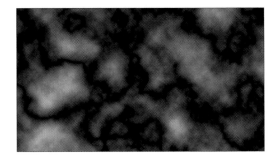

STEP 4. Defining the Flame Shapes

With the foreground color still set to black, choose the Brush Tool from the toolbox. Click on the down arrow on the Options bar to open the Brush Preset Picker, drag the Master Diameter slider to set the brush size to 10, and then close the Brush Preset Picker. (If necessary, you can also display the Brushes Palette, click on Brush Tip Shape at the left, and then drag the Spacing slider so you get a solid line rather than the dot pattern from the previous project.) Identify the areas of flame shape that you want to keep, and use the Brush Tool to color around them in black, more clearly defining the flame shape.

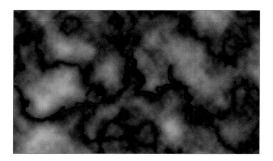

STEP 5. Removing Unwanted Areas

Choose the Lasso Tool from the toolbox and use it to select the areas of texture above the flame shape that you want to eliminate from the image. With the foreground color still set to black, use the Paint Bucket Tool or press Alt+Del to fill the selection with black.

Choose Select > Deselect to remove the selection marquee.

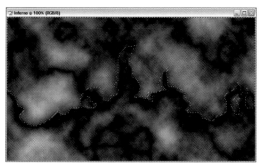
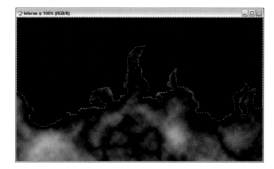

STEP 6. Adding a Gradient Layer

Click on the Create a New Layer button in the Layers Palette to add a new layer named Layer 1. With the default foreground and background colors still selected, choose the Gradient Tool from the toolbox. Click on the Linear Gradient button on the Options bar, choose the Foreground to Background gradient from the Gradient Presets, and then drag from the top to the bottom of the image window to apply a gradient to the new layer, as shown here.

STEP 7. Blending the Gradient Layer

With Layer 1 still selected in the Layers Palette, open the Layer Style drop-down list in the upper-left corner of the Layers Palette, and then click on Soft Light to make the lower portion of the image brighter.

Click on the Palette menu button in the upper-right corner of the Layers Palette, and then click on Merge Down to merge the layers.

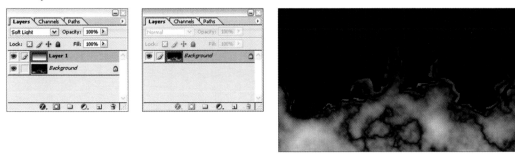

STEP 8. Coloring the Flames

Now change the gradient colors to black, red, and yellow to make the flames look realistic. Select Image > Adjustments > Gradient Map from the menu bar. Click on the gradient in the Gradient Used for Grayscale Mapping box of the Gradient Map dialog box to open the Gradient Editor dialog box.

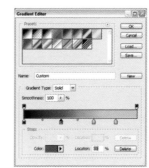

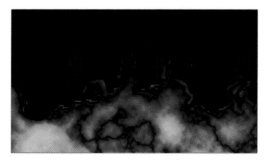

Click on the first gradient preset in the Presets area if it is not already selected, and then create two more color stops at the bottom of the gradient preview to include additional gradient colors. To set up a stop, click on the bottom of the gradient preview, and then click on the Color box at the bottom of the dialog box to open the Color Picker and choose the color for that stop.

Double-click on the far-right color stop to change its color, and then drag it left to move it to the position shown here. (You can delete a color stop by dragging it off the bottom of the preview.)

Click on OK to close the Gradient Editor dialog box, and then click on OK again to apply the gradient.

STEP 9. Completing the Flame Image

Choose the Rectangular Marquee Tool from the toolbox and drag to select the portion of the image that you want to include in your final composition.

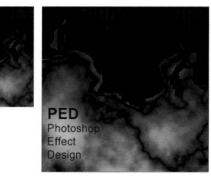

Select Image > Crop from the menu bar to delete the areas outside the selection. You can then add text and other elements to the image as desired.

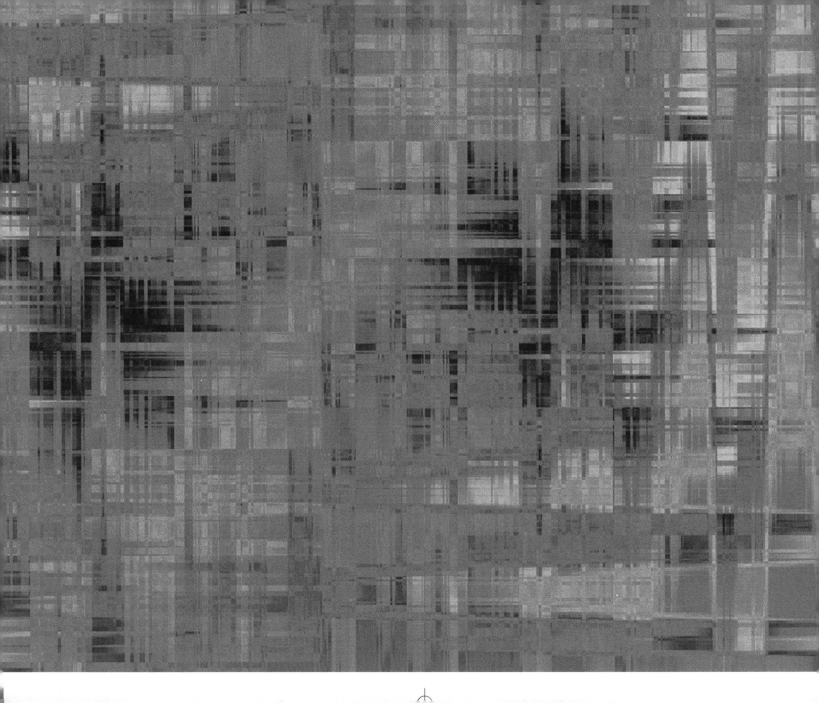

Index

Numerics

3D effects
cloud effects, 73, 87, 89
column effects, 67
deep hole effects, 104
metallic sphere effects, 188–195
overlapped squares, 17
wire frame bridge effects, 212–217
90 CW command (Image menu, Rotate), 50, 65–66, 113–114

A

Add a Layer Style button (Layers Palette), 95
Add Layer Mask button (Layers Palette), 139
Add Noise command (Filter menu, Noise), 7, 16, 19, 38, 53, 112, 150, 200
Adjustments command (Image menu)
Auto Color, 177
Curves, 6, 30, 54, 77, 105, 133, 139
Desaturate, 156–157, 162
Gradient Map, 154, 235
Hue/Saturation, 39, 64, 94–95, 123, 134–135
Invert, 136, 139, 156
Levels, 9, 48, 84, 94, 122, 125, 127, 132, 151
Photo Filter, 54
Variations, 177, 194
alignment, evenly spaced text, 155
Artistic command (Filter menu)
Cutout, 6, 94, 181, 222
Dry Brush, 52, 222
Palette Knife, 49, 192
Smudge Stick, 134
artwork effects, 132–145
Auto Color command (Image menu, Adjustments), 177

B

barcode window effects, 8–9
Bas Relief command (Filter menu, Sketch), 73
bead effects, 38–43
black borders, 135–136
blending options, 21–22
cloud effects, 88
Color Burn, 145, 167
Color Dodge, 54
Darken, 133
edges, 126
Lighten, 66
Linear Burn, 42
Linear Light, 103
Multiply, 63, 105
Outer Glow, 194
Overlay, 95–96, 183
Screen, 66, 75, 77
shadow effects, 42
text, 21, 23
blue gradients, sea effects, 73
Blur command (Filter menu)
Gaussian Blur, 42, 50, 52, 54, 62, 88, 150, 152, 188, 222
Motion Blur, 54, 67, 76
Radial Blur, 126–127
Smart Blur, 17, 19, 30
borders, 56
black, 135–136
resizing, 136
white, 136–137
brick effects, broken wall texture, 16–23
bridge effects, 212–217
brightness, correcting, photo restoration, 176
Brush Tool
Brush Presets Panel, 62, 102
Brush Tip Shape option, 213
Shape Dynamics option, 214
Spatter 46 Pixels, 163–164
Special Effect Brushes, 140

burning flame effects, 232–235
buttons
    Add a Layer Style (Layers Palette), 95
    Add Layer Mask (Layers Palette), 139
    Commit Any Current Edits, 97
    Create a New Layer (Layers Palette), 7, 20, 62
    Create New Fill (Layers Palette), 20, 30
    Create New Style (Styles Palette), 41
    Default Foreground and Background Colors, 7, 28, 40
    Delete (Layers Palette), 9
    Foreground Color, 20, 73, 78
    Geometry Options (Line Tool), 116
    Gradient Color (Gradient Map), 20
    New Effect Layer (Filter Gallery), 49
    Randomize, 4

C

Channels command (Window menu), 188–189
Character and Paragraph Palette, 97
Character Palette, 10
circle effects, 188
Clear Layer Style option (Layers Palette), 136
Clone Stamp Tool, 178
cloud effects
    3D, 73, 87, 89
    black and white texture, 138
    black cloud channels, 86
    cube effects, 122
    darkened areas, blending and softening, 88
    flame effects, 232
    particles, 16
    repeating, 16, 48, 50, 62, 86, 103
    sea effects, 72
    shadows in, adjusting, 48
    shapes, deleting, 87
    shaping, 85
    sharpened, 84, 122
Clouds command (Filter menu, Render), 16, 48, 50, 62, 72, 84, 138, 232

collage effects, 162–171
color
    color correction, 30
    color stops, 154
    cyan, 39
    flame effects, 235
    image color, photo restoration, 177
    inverting, 29
    mosaic, sharpening, 39
    restoration, 142
    softened, 30
Color Burn blend mode, 145, 167
Color Dodge blend mode, 54
Color Halftone command (Filter menu, Pixelate), 39
Color Range command (Select menu), 190
column effects, 67
Commit Any Current Edits button, 97
copying
    layers, 65
    selections, 193
Create a New Layer button (Layers Palette), 7, 20, 62
Create New Fill button (Layers Palette), 20, 30
Create New Style button (Styles Palette), 41
Crop command (Image menu), 5–6, 40, 79, 115, 189, 195, 226, 235
Crystallize command (Filter menu, Pixelate), 54, 104, 112
cube effects, 122–127
Curves command (Image menu, Adjustments), 6, 30, 54, 77, 105, 133, 139
Cutout command (Filter menu, Artistic), 6, 94, 181, 222
cutout effects, 94–97
cyan color, 39
cyberspace effects, 4–11

D

dancing light effects, 28–33
Darken blend mode, 133
deep hole effects, 102–107
Default Foreground and Background Colors button, 7, 28, 40

Define Brush Preset command (Edit menu), 213
Define Pattern command (Edit menu), 190, 224
Delete button (Layers Palette), 9
Desaturate command (Image menu, Adjustments), 156–157, 162
Deselect command (Select menu), 96–97, 135, 166, 188, 191, 195, 204, 233
Despeckle command (Filter menu, Noise), 177
Difference Clouds command (Filter menu, Render), 48, 72, 137, 232
Direct Selection Tool, 214
directional lighting, 191
Displace command (Filter menu, Distort), 50, 64, 136–137
Displace map images, 49
Distort command (Filter menu)
　　Displace, 50, 64, 136–137
　　Wave, 124–125
dots
　　bead effects, 38
　　skyscraper effects, 112
Dry Brush command (Filter menu, Artistic), 52, 222

E

edges
　　blended, 126
　　Find Edges command (Filter menu), 125
　　glowing, 151, 201
　　sharpened, 17
　　softened, 17
Edit menu commands
　　Define Brush Preset, 213
　　Define Pattern, 190, 224
　　Fade Lighting Effects, 18
　　Fade Unsharp Mask, 113
　　Fade Wave, 124
　　Fill, 190, 225
　　Free Transform, 97, 103, 136
　　Transform
　　　　Rotate 90 CCW, 6, 107
　　　　Rotate 180, 137, 168
　　　　Scale, 153, 204
Elliptical Marquee Tool, 188
engraved collage effects, 162–171
enlarged images, 39
enlarged text, 21
evenly spaced text, 155
Eyedropper Tool, 107

F

facial contour, photo restoration, 178–181
Fade Lighting Effects command (Edit menu), 18
Fade Unsharp Mask command (Edit menu), 113
Fade Wave command (Edit menu), 124
Feather command (Select menu), 74–75
fiber effects, 52
File menu commands
　　New, 150, 165, 188, 200, 232
　　Open, 132, 162
Fill command (Edit menu), 190, 225
Filter Gallery, 49
filter layers, 49
Filter menu commands
　　Artistic
　　　　Cutout, 6, 94, 181, 222
　　　　Dry Brush, 52, 222
　　　　Palette Knife, 49, 192
　　　　Smudge Stick, 134
　　Blur
　　　　Gaussian Blur, 42, 50, 52, 54, 62, 88, 150, 152, 188, 222
　　　　Motion Blur, 54, 67, 76–77
　　　　Radial Blur, 126–127
　　　　Smart Blur, 17, 19, 30
　　Distort
　　　　Displace, 50, 64, 136–137
　　　　Wave, 124–125

Liquify, 179
Noise
  Add Noise, 7, 16, 19, 38, 53, 112, 150, 200
  Despeckle, 177
  Median, 29, 104, 132, 192
Other
  Maximum, 17
  Minimum, 16
Pixelate
  Color Halftone, 39
  Crystallize, 54, 104, 112
  Mosaic, 38, 123, 151
  Pointillize, 28
Render
  Clouds, 16, 48, 50, 62, 72, 84, 138, 232
  Difference Clouds, 48, 72, 137, 232
  Fibers, 52
  Lighting, 18, 152
  Lighting Effects, 87, 104, 191
Sharpen, Unsharp Mask, 17, 29, 104, 113, 133
Sketch
  Bas Relief, 73
  Graphic Pen, 50
  Plaster, 138
Stylize
  Find Edges, 125
  Glowing Edges, 151, 201
  Wind, 65, 113
Texture
  Grain, 28
  Patchwork, 201
Find Edges command (Filter menu, Stylize), 125
fine line removal, photo restoration, 178
fire effects, 232–235
flame effects, 232–235
flower bouquet effects, 141
Foreground Color button, 20

Forward Warp Tool, 180
Free Transform command (Edit menu), 9, 21–22, 65, 73, 97, 103, 136
Freeze Mask Tool, 179
frosted glass effects, 49
fuzziness effects, 190

G

Gaussian Blur command (Filter menu, Blur), 42, 50, 52, 54, 62, 88, 150, 152, 188, 222
Geometry Options button (Line Tool), 116
glass effects, 49
Glowing Edges command (Filter menu, Stylize), 151, 201
glowing effects, 194
Gradient Editor Panel, 4
Gradient Map command (Image menu, Adjustments), 154, 235
Gradient Tool
  Gradient Color button, 4
  Gradient Preset Panel, 113
  Linear Gradient button, 4
gradients
  blue, sea effects, 73
  color, selecting, 20
Grain command (Filter menu, Texture), 28
graininess, removing, photo restoration, 177
Graphic Pen command (Filter menu, Sketch), 50

H

Healing Brush Tool, 178
hole effects, 102–107
Horizontal Type Tool, 10–11, 23, 43, 107, 127, 195
Hue/Saturation command (Image menu, Adjustments), 39, 64, 94–95, 123, 134–135
Hue/Saturation option (Layers palette), 33

I

Image menu commands
    Adjustments
        Auto Color, 177
        Curves, 6, 30, 54, 77, 105, 133, 139
        Desaturate, 156–157, 162
        Gradient Map, 154, 235
        Hue/Saturation, 39, 64, 94–95, 123, 134–135
        Invert, 136, 139, 156
        Levels, 9, 48, 84, 94, 122, 125, 127, 132, 151
        Photo Filter, 54
        Variations, 177, 194
    Crop, 5–6, 40, 79, 115, 189, 195, 225, 235
    Image Size, 5, 8, 39, 132
    Rotate Canvas, 90 CW, 50, 65–66, 113–114
Image Size command (Image menu), 5, 8, 39, 132
images
    brightening, 30
    Displace map, 49
    enlarging, 39
    sharpened, 30
    softened, 19, 30
inkblot effects, 138
Inverse command (Select menu), 189
Invert command (Image menu, Adjustments), 136, 139, 156

L

large colored particles, 28
Lasso Tool, 233
Layer Visibility icon (Layers palette), 41, 63
Layers command (Window menu), 189, 215
Layers Palette
    Add a Layer Style button, 95
    Add Layer Mask button, 139
    Blend Mode, 21–22
        Color Burn, 145, 167
        Color Dodge, 54
        Darken, 133
        Lighten, 66

        Linear Burn, 42
        Linear Light, 103
        Multiply, 53, 63, 105
        Outer Glow, 194
        Overlay, 95–96, 183
        Screen, 66, 75, 77
    Clear Layer Style option, 136
    copying layers, 65
    Create a New Layer button, 7, 20, 62
    Create New Fill button, 20
    Delete button, 9
    Hue/Saturation option, 32–33
    Layer Visibility icon, 41, 63
    Merge Down option, 234
    merged layers, 64
Levels command (Image menu, Adjustments), 9, 48, 84, 94, 122, 125, 127, 132, 151
Lighten blend mode, 66
lighting effects
    dancing light effects, 28–33
    faded, 18
Lighting Effects command (Filter menu, Render), 18, 87, 104, 152, 191
Line Tool, 116
Linear Burn blend mode, 42
Linear Gradient button (Gradient Tool), 4
Linear Light blend mode, 103
lines, vertical, 62, 64
Liquify command (Filter menu), 179
Load Selection command (Select menu), 213

M

Magic Wand Tool, 9, 40
mask thumbnails, 33
Maximum command (Filter menu, Other), 17
Median command (Filter menu, Noise), 29, 104, 132, 192
Merge Down option (Layers Palette), 234
merged layers, 64
metallic sphere effects, 188–195

Minimum command (Filter menu, Other command), 16
Mode command (Image menu), 132
molted texture effects, 140
mosaic color, sharpening, 39
Mosaic command (Filter menu, Pixelate), 38, 123, 151
mosaic effects, 200–207
Motion Blur command (Filter menu, Blur), 54, 67, 76
Move Tool, 116
multi-colored particles, 28
Multiply blend mode, 53, 63, 105

N

Navigator Palette, 153, 212
Nearest Neighbor resample image option, 8
New command (File menu), 165, 188, 200, 232
New Effect Layer button (Filter Gallery), 49
new network window, creating
    bead effects, 38
    brick effects, broken wall texture, 16
    cyberspace effects, 4
    dancing light effects, 28
    path effects, 62
    rough drawing style effects, 48
    sea effects, 72
    sky effects, 84
    skyscraper effects, 112
Noise command (Filter menu)
    Add Noise, 7, 16, 19, 38, 53, 112, 150, 200
    Despeckle, 177
    Median, 29, 104, 132, 192

O

Open command (File menu), 132
Other command (Filter menu)
    Maximum, 17
    Minimum, 16
Outer Glow blend mode, 194

overlapped squares, 17
overlapped text, 22
Overlay blend mode, 95–96, 183

P

Paint Bucket Tool, 96, 165, 212
Palette Knife command (Filter menu, Artistic), 49, 192
particles
    cloud effects, 16
    colors in, mixing, 29
    crystallized, 104
    large colored, 28
    multi-colored, 28
    shiny, 29
Patchwork command (Filter menu, Texture), 201
path effects, 62–67
Paths command (Window menu), 215
pattern effects, 190
pen sketch effects, 50
Pen Tool, 206, 214
Pencil Tool, 224
Photo Filter command (Image menu, Adjustments), 54
photo restoration
    brightness, correcting, 176
    facial contour, 178–181
    fine lines, removing, 178
    graininess, removing, 177
    image color, adjusting, 177
photographs, blurring, 222
pipe effects, 150–157
Pixelate command (Filter menu)
    Color Halftone, 39
    Crystallize, 54, 104, 112
    Mosaic, 38, 123, 151
    Pointillize, 28, 38
Plaster command (Filter menu, Sketch), 138
Pointillize command (Filter menu, Pixelate), 28
Polygonal Lasso Tool, 95
Poster Edges thumbnail, 49

R

Radian Blur command (Filter menu, Blur), 126–127
Randomize button, 4
Raw Image command (Window menu), 162–164
rays, sun rays, sea effects, 76–78
rectangles, 167, 215
Rectangular Marquee Tool, 5, 8, 40, 64, 96–97
Red option (Texture Channel), 18, 152, 191
reflection, 127
Render command (Filter menu)
    Clouds, 16, 48, 50, 62, 72, 84, 138, 232
    Difference Clouds, 48, 72, 137, 232
    Fibers, 52
    Lighting Effects, 18, 87, 104, 152, 191
Resample Image option, 8
restoration, color, 142
RGB Color command (Image menu, Mode), 132
ripple effects, sea effects, 74–75
Rotate 90 CCW command (Edit menu, Transform), 6, 107
Rotate 180 command (Edit menu, Transform), 137, 168
rotating
    layers, 168
    text, 56
rough drawing style effects, 48–57

S

Scale command (Edit menu, Transform), 153, 204
Screen blend mode, 66, 75, 77
sea effects, 72–79
Select menu commands
    Color Range, 190
    Deselect, 96–97, 135, 166, 188, 191, 195, 204, 224, 233
    Feather, 74–75
    Inverse, 189
    Load Selection, 213

shadow effects
    blended, 42
    in clouds, 48
    color shadows, 42
    metallic sphere effects, 193
Shape Dynamics option (Brushes Palette), 214
Sharpen command (Filter menu), 17, 29, 104, 113, 133
sharpened cloud effects, 84, 122
sharpened edges, 17
sharpened images, 30
sharpened mosaic color, 39
shiny particles, 29
Single Row Marquee Tool, 7
size of text, adjusting, 22
Sketch command (Filter menu)
    Bas Relief, 73
    Graphic Pen, 50
    Plaster, 138
sky effects, 84–89
skyscraper effects, 112–117
small font size, 10
Smart Blur command (Filter menu, Blur), 17, 19, 30
Smudge Stick command (Filter menu, Artistic), 134
softened cloud effects, 88
softened colors, 30
softened edges, 17
softened images, 19, 30
solid stripes, 96
Spatter 46 Pixels brush, 163–164
Special Effect Brushes, 140
speckles, blurred effects, 150
spheres, metallic effects, 188–195
straight vertical gradients, 5
stripes
    solid, 96
    vertical, 7, 54, 96, 165
Styles Palette, 41

Stylize command (Filter menu)
    Find Edges, 125
    Glowing Edges, 151, 201
    Wind, 65, 113
sun rays, sea effects, 76–78

T

text
    blending, 21, 23
    enlarging, 21
    evenly spaced, 155
    individual letters, moving, 155
    overlapped, 22
    rotating, 56
    size, adjusting, 22
Texture command (Filter menu)
    Grain, 28
    Patchwork, 201
thumbnails
    mask, 33
    Poster Edges, 49
tile effects, 202
titles, entering
    bead effects, 43
    brick effects, 21–23
    cube effects, 127
    cyberspace effects, 10
    dancing light effects, 32
    path effects, 67
    rough drawing text styles, 57
    sea effects, 79
    sky effects, 89
    skyscraper effects, 117
Tolerance option (Magic Wand Tool), 40
Transform command (Edit menu)
    Rotate 90 CCW, 6, 107
    Rotate 180, 137, 168
    Scale, 153, 204
transparency, 204

U

Unsharp Mask command (Filter menu, Sharpen), 17, 29, 104, 113, 133

V

Variations command (Image menu, Adjustments), 177, 194
vertical lines, 62, 64
vertical stripes, 7, 54, 96, 165

W

Warp Tool, 180
Water Drop style icon (Styles Palette), 41
water ripples, sea effects, 74–75
Wave command (Filter menu, Distort), 124–125
white backgrounds, 40
white borders, 136–137
white foregrounds, 78
Wind command (Filter menu, Stylize), 65, 113
Window menu commands
    Channels, 188–189
    Layers, 189, 215
    Paths, 215
    Raw Image, 162–164
wire frame bridge effects, 212–217
woodcut effects, 94–97

Z

Zoom Tool, 179–180

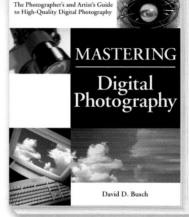

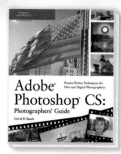

License Agreement/Notice of Limited Warranty